Nancy Garden's Annie on My Mind: A Discussion Guide

David Bruce

Published by David Bruce, 2022.

NANCY GARDEN'S ANNIE ON MY MIND: A DISCUSSION GUIDE

First edition. November 1, 2022.

Copyright © 2022 David Bruce.

ISBN: 979-8215205938

Written by David Bruce.

Table of Contents

Dedication

Dedicated to My Mother

Josephine Bruce, my mother, died at 7:40 p.m. Saturday, 14 June 2003 at Hickory Creek Nursing Center in The Plains.

She could have died a few weeks earlier at Doctors Hospital in Nelsonville, but I made the decision to have her connected to a machine that would breathe for her. In doing this, I went against her wishes that she had very clearly expressed to me previously.

As it happened, this was most likely the right thing to do. She was connected to the breathing machine for less than 12 hours and was then able to breathe on her own until she died Saturday. It was possible that she would have had to stay connected to the breathing machine for the rest of her life.

She forgave me for my decision.

In the additional weeks that remained to her, the most important thing we did together was to write letters to all of her children. The basic message of each letter was the same: I love you and I know that you love me.

When she died, all of her children were with her.

She knew she was dying. When I saw her that morning, I knew that she was very ill and I told her that this might be the day she died. When her doctor arrived, he let her know that she would most likely not survive.

This is exactly the way it should be. If I were dying, I would want to know.

She was not afraid of death. She knew that it was time, and I think that she welcomed it. Like the old song says, as a Christian, she was wearing her traveling shoes. However, like most of us, she was probably afraid that dying might be painful.

Her dying was not painful. Doctors are humane, and pain management is now an advanced art. Morphine took away the pain.

Her dying was fairly quick. Her doctor told me that she would probably die within 12 to 24 hours. From the time he told me that to the time she died took seven and a half hours.

The seven and a half hours were a misery, but to wait 12 to 24 hours for her to die would have been an extended stay in Hell.

When she died, one of her sons was holding her right hand and one of her daughters was holding her left hand. Her other children were gathered around her.

Her death was quiet. The time between each breath grew longer and longer and soon there was no next breath.

One minute she was alive and breathing. The next minute—with no change in her expression—she was dead.

While she was dying, we played her favorite gospel and country music on her stereo. She died as her favorite singer, John Denver, was singing about going home again.

People who live in nursing homes tend to have few opportunities to do good deeds that involve money, but one thing she did was to send flowers to the Hickory Creek Nursing Center kitchen to thank the kitchen workers because she liked the food.

People who live in nursing homes tend to have few possessions. Her most valuable possessions were her music CDs, which—as she requested—her children divided among themselves.

An additional possession, which is valuable in educating future doctors, was her body. Months before she died, she donated her body to the Ohio University College of Osteopathic Medicine. That night, very quickly after she died, her body was taken away to the college.

That was her final good deed. Her gift will allow a future doctor to be taught how to help people.

People treated her well, both in life and in death.

As a very ill patient, she spent time in O'Bleness Hospital in Athens and in Doctors Hospital in Nelsonville. At each hospital, she received excellent care.

Of course, she spent much time at Hickory Creek Nursing Center in The Plains. No one who works there is paid even half what his or her work is worth. In this society, a bad actor in a bad TV series can make hundreds of thousands of dollars a year while the people doing very much more valuable work in nursing homes make very much less money.

Because of my mother, I see the value of such government programs as Social Security, Medicare, and Medicaid. I see how valuable they are in helping provide care for old people. If anything, more money should be poured into these programs and more money should be poured into the government programs that help children. (Healthy adults such as myself should work and pay the taxes that support these programs.)

As my mother lay dying, and after, Hickory Creek Nursing Center treated her children well. They provided a private room for her, one big enough for all seven of her children and a few other relatives to sit in. The kitchen workers provided coffee, tea, water, and food. Some of the Hickory Creek employees hugged me and said I was a good son. After she died, we were given all the time we wanted to say goodbye. We also made use of the chapel.

Many people helped my mother and took care of her and comforted her children. She was much loved—and not just by her children.

Cover Photograph for Nancy Garden's *Annie on My Mind*: A Discussion Guide

Model: Victoria Borodonova

https://pixabay.com/photos/kiss-lgbt-girls-lesbian-lesbians-2897401/

https://www.instagram.com/victoriaborodinova/

https://www.facebook.com/victoria.borodinova

https://pixabay.com/users/victoria_borodinova-6314823/

Educate Yourself

Read Like A Wolf Eats

Be Excellent to Each Other

Books Then, Books Now, Books Forever

Preface

The purpose of this book is educational. I enjoy reading Nancy Garden's *Annie on My Mind*, and I believe that it is an excellent book for young adults (and for old adults such as myself) to read.

This book contains many questions about Nancy Garden's *Annie on My Mind* and their answers. I hope that teachers of young adults will find it useful as a guide for discussions. It can also be used for short writing assignments. Students can answer selected questions from this little guide orally or in one or more paragraphs.

I hope to encourage teachers to teach Nancy Garden's *Annie on My Mind* and I hope to lessen the time needed for teachers to prepare to teach this book.

This book uses many short quotations from Nancy Garden's *Annie on My Mind*. This use is consistent with fair use:

§ 107. Limitations on exclusive rights: Fair use

Release date: 2004-04-30

Notwithstanding the provisions of sections 106 and 106A, the fair use of a copyrighted work, including such use by reproduction in copies or phonorecords or by any other means specified by that section, for purposes such as criticism, comment, news reporting, teaching (including multiple copies for classroom use), scholarship, or research, is not an infringement of copyright. In determining whether the use made of a work in any particular case is a fair use the factors to be considered shall include —

(1) the purpose and character of the use, including whether such use is of a commercial nature or is for nonprofit educational purposes;

(2) the nature of the copyrighted work;

(3) the amount and substantiality of the portion used in relation to the copyrighted work as a whole; and

(4) the effect of the use upon the potential market for or value of the copyrighted work.

The fact that a work is unpublished shall not itself bar a finding of fair use if such finding is made upon consideration of all the above factors.

Pages Before Chapter 1

What do we learn about Annie and Liza in these pages?

• These pages tell us that Liza — Eliza Winthrop — is a freshman architecture student at MIT.

• Liza is 5-foot-3-inches tall, and she has short, brown hair.

• Liza is thinking about Annie even though she hadn't meant to think about Annie; instead, she had meant to begin writing a paper about the architecture of the famous USAmerican architect Frank Lloyd Wright.

• Liza begins writing a letter to Annie, although she thinks that she will not mail it — at least not until she thinks about how she came to know Annie and what happened afterward.

• The feeling of these pages is one of sadness. Liza is uncertain about what she wants to do.

• We learn that Liza had written a letter to Annie earlier — when Annie was in her second week of music school — but that Liza has not written since. Now Annie — who has been writing — says that she will not write again until Liza writes her another letter first.

• Liza lives in Brooklyn Heights, New York, while Annie lives in Manhattan.

Who is Frank Lloyd Wright?

Frank Lloyd Wright is perhaps the United States' greatest architect. One of his most famous buildings is Fallingwater, a house in Pennsylvania that is partly built over a waterfall.

Chapter 1

How do Liza and Annie meet?

• Liza and Annie have what movie critic Roger Ebert called a Meet Cute. A "Meet Cute" occurs whenever two characters in a movie — usually a romantic comedy — have a meeting that is cute in some way. For example, in *Notting Hill*, Julia Roberts and Hugh Grant meet first in Hugh Grant's book store (which sells only travel books), then later meet again when Hugh Grant crashes into Julia Roberts while carrying a large cup of orange juice, which he spills all over her.

• In *Annie on My Mind*, Eliza has gone to the Metropolitan Museum of Art to think about a solar-house project. There she hears Annie singing, and when Annie stops, Eliza tells her not to. They introduce themselves, like each other, and pretend to joust with one another like medieval knights.

• Liza and Annie do have fun together.

• The two exchange telephone numbers and addresses.

Write a character analysis of Liza based on what you learn from her first meeting with Annie.

• Liza's last name is Winthrop.

• Liza makes the first move — she speaks first to Annie.

• Usually, Liza likes to be alone in the museum, but she finds that she doesn't mind if Annie tags along with her.

• Liza listens to her English teacher, Ms. Widmer. She begins her story with the first important or exciting incident — that incident turns out to be meeting Annie, so we know that Annie is important to Eliza.

• Liza likes going to the Metropolitan Museum of Art, where she visits the Temple of Dendur and the American Wing.

• Liza likes Annie in part because Annie is enthusiastic about what she finds in the museum. (Liza does think that Annie is a little strange.)

- Liza does play-joust with Annie, but only after noticing that the only people around who can see her are a couple of small boys.

- Liza almost calls Annie beautiful to her face.

Write a character analysis of Annie based on what you learn from her first meeting with Liza.

- Annie's last name is Kenyon.

- Annie likes going to the Metropolitan Museum of Art

- Annie likes to sing and to play-act. She is creative.

- Annie wears a cape — possibly an artistic article of clothing.

- Annie has long black hair.

- Annie thinks that Liza is "bright and clear" (14), while she is somber" (14).

Compare and contrast Liza and Annie.

- Both are young girls. Both are 17, and both are seniors in high school. (I say "high school girls" and "college women.")

- As we learned earlier, before chapter 1, both will go to college.

- Both are artistic. Eliza wants to be an architect; Annie sings and is involved in music.

- Annie is less inhibited than Eliza. Annie can and will play-joust if she wants to. Eliza can do this, but she is self-conscious at first.

- Both go to museums.

What are the Metropolitan Museum of Art, the Temple of Dendur, and the American Wing?

The Metropolitan Museum of Art

The Metropolitan Museum of Art was founded in 1870 and houses many important works of art. It is in New York City's Central Park. The Museum includes Rembrandts and Vermeers as well as Impressionist and Post-Impressionist paintings. It also has a fine collection of Islamic art. In addition, it houses many other collections, including a collection of medieval armor and weapons.

The Temple of Dendur

In about 15 B.C.E., the Temple of Dendur, a shrine to the goddess Isis, was built. Today, it is part of the museum's Egyptian collection. In 1963, the temple was dismantled and moved because of the new Aswan High Dam, which raised the water of the Nile River so high that the water would have submerged the temple. In 1965, the temple was offered as a gift from Egypt to the United States.

The American Wing

According to the website of the Metropolitan Museum of Art, "Ever since its establishment in 1870 the Museum has acquired important examples of American Art. A separate 'American Wing' building to display the domestic arts of the seventeenth–early nineteenth centuries opened in 1924; paintings galleries and an enclosed sculpture court were added in 1980."

Chapter 2

What do we learn about Liza in chapter 2?

• Liza has a playful brother named Chad, who is two years younger than her.

• Liza is President of the Student Council.

• Liza has a sense of responsibility, but a sense of responsibility that is not well enough developed yet. She does check out the ear-piercing clinic, but she decides that it is sanitary enough and lets it continue doing business.

• Liza is a straight-A student.

• Liza lives in a good neighborhood and attends a private school. Her neighborhood is middle class or perhaps upper middle class. The wage-earners living in the brownstone apartments are doctors, lawyers, and professors. (On p. 48, we find out that Liza's father is an engineer who attended MIT.)

Write a character analysis of Chad, Liza's younger brother.

• Chad is 15, two years younger than Liza.

• Chad and Liza have a playful relationship. Liza and Chad end up throwing leaves at each other in chapter 2.

• Chad has been memorizing the Powers of Congress and is surprised that Liza doesn't remember them. He wonders what is the point of memorizing something at age 15 if you will forget it by age 17?

• Chad is perceptive. He says that Liza must be in love. As it turns out, this is true. (This is a good example of foreshadowing.)

What is foreshadowing, and what example of it do we see in Chapter 2?

The 6th edition of *A Handbook to Literature* by C. Hugh Holman and William Harmon defines "foreshadowing" in this way: "The presentation of material in a work in such a way that later events are prepared for" (201).

Here are a couple of other definitions:

Foreshadowing is the use of hints or clues to suggest what will happen later in literature.

Source:

http://www.tnellen.com/cybereng/lit_terms/
foreshadowing.html

Date Accessed: 2 October 2011

Definition: A literary device used to hint at events that will follow later in the story, sometimes generating feelings of anxiety or suspense. Anton Chekhov once said that "if there is a gun hanging on the wall in the first act, it must fire in the last." That remark captures the essence of foreshadowing.

Source:

http://contemporarylit.about.com/library/
bldef-foreshadowing

Of course, plays also contain foreshadowing.

Chad is perceptive. He says that Liza must be in love. As it turns out, this is true. (This is a good example of foreshadowing.)

What is the financial situation of Foster Academy? Who is Mr. Piccolo?

• Foster Academy — a private school — is in financial trouble. That is why they have consulted a professional fundraiser and started a "major campaign" (18).

• The fundraising campaign is significant because the fundraisers will want to avoid any sign of scandal — a scandal could result in people not wanting to donate money to Foster Academy.

• Mr. Piccolo is on the fundraising committee. He is also a parent whose daughter — Jennifer — attends Foster Academy. Both Mr. Piccolo and Jennifer are like the musical instrument they are named after: tall and thin.

• A piccolo plays an important part in John Philip Sousa's "Stars and Stripes Forever." A piccolo is a musical instrument that is a small flute that produces music an octave higher than a standard flute.

Write a character analysis of Sally Jarrell.

• We learn that Sally Jarrell later changes, but that in this chapter she is a true original who goes her own way.

• Sally Jarrell is a go-getter, apparently, who doesn't mind setting up her own ear-piercing clinic.

• Unfortunately, she hasn't thought things through. A number of girls whose ears she pierces end up holding bloody tissues to their ears in various classes.

• Neither Sally nor Liza are in cliques.

• Liza says about Sally, "In a world of people who seemed to have come out of duplicating machines, Sally Jarrell was no one's copy, not that fall anyway" (19).

Did Liza act properly when she learned about Sally Jarrell's ear-piercing clinic?

• No, she should have been more responsible. Sally is not a doctor, and it's best to have a professional do body mutilation — uh, ear piercing.

• Still, Liza does consider the situation carefully and make decisions, although she makes the wrong decisions — the decisions that the procedure is sanitary enough and that Sally should be allowed to continue piercing ears.

• Jennifer Piccolo is hurt when her ears are pierced — this should be reason enough for Liza to stop Sally from piercing more ears.

• Liza does like Sally a lot — that may be clouding her judgment.

If you feel like doing research, investigate a few of the problems that can result from body piercing. (Do not plagiarize.)

Most body piercing is done in the earlobes, and most people do not have problems arising from piercings. Both men and women get body piercings in various parts of their bodies.

Piercing the earlobes is usually safe, although problems can arise when other parts of the ear are pierced because the needle goes through cartilage. Piercings through cartilage are more likely to become infected than piercings through earlobes.

The most common problem from piercings is infection of the pierced site.

Diseases can also be spread through piercing the body if a sterile technique is not used. The diseases that can be transmitted include hepatitis B or hepatitis C, tuberculosis, syphilis, HIV, and blood infections (sepsis).

In addition, the person having the piercing may discover that he or she is allergic to the metal used in the jewelry displayed in the pierced body part.

Write a character analysis of Ms. Stevenson.

• Ms. Stevenson teaches art and is faculty advisor to student council.

• Ms. Stevenson is strict but fair.

• Ms. Stevenson recognizes that Sally's piercing of ears is not a good idea.

• Ms. Stevenson does have pierced ears — but a doctor pierced her ears. Also, she was in college when her ears were pierced.

Chapters 2-3

Write a character analysis of Mrs. Poindexter.

- The name "Poindexter" is a hint that this is an unsympathetic character. A "poindexter" is a nerd.
- Mrs. Poindexter believes in responsibility. She wants Liza to be a role model for other students.
- Mrs. Poindexter does not have a nicely decorated office. It has shades of brown and is unattractive.
- She is stubby and gray-haired and always looks as if she has a pain somewhere.
- She cares very much about Foster Academy.
- She feels that Liza did not do her duty when she allowed Sally Jarrell to keep piercing the ears of students.
- She makes Liza explain her actions, and she makes Liza feel guilty.
- Mrs. Poindexter is really worried about the school, and she desperately wants the fundraising effort to be successful. She is worried about anything that would negatively impact that fundraising effort.
- Mrs. Poindexter is worried that Mr. Piccolo may not help with the fundraising effort since his daughter had to leave school and go home after getting her ears pierced.
- A disciplinary hearing will take place for both Liza and Sally.

Chapter 3

What is the reporting rule?

• The reporting rule is Foster Academy's honor code. It has three parts:

1) If you do something wrong, you are supposed to report yourself.

2) If you see someone doing something wrong, you are supposed to tell that person to report him- or herself.

3) If that person does not report him- or herself, you are supposed to report him or her.

• Most faculty and students think that the reporting rule does not work. Liza even spoke out against it when she was elected Student Council President. Mrs. Poindexter disagrees.

Who is Ms. Baxter?

• Ms. Baxter is Mrs. Poindexter's toady.

• She teaches the Bible as Literature to juniors and she tells young students Bible stories.

• She has dyed red hair.

• She is Mrs. Poindexter's administrative assistant.

• They are not equals; Ms. Baxter is clearly subservient to Mrs. Poindexter.

Write a character analysis of Liza's mom based on what you learn in chapter 3.

• She is a good person. Both Liza and Chad can talk to her. Even if they are wrong, their Mom can help them sort out their problem without making them feel like worms.

- She makes lots of cookies — perhaps as a result of feeling guilty because she is not a stay-at-home Mom. However, no one except herself expects her to be a stay-at-home Mom.

- She is active in the neighborhood association — she attends its meetings.

- She leaves notes as needed for members of her family.

What do we learn from Annie and Liza's telephone conversation?

- Both are nervous, but both like each other.

- They set up a kind of date. They are going to go to the Cloisters together.

- This time, Annie makes the first move. She calls, and she asks Liza to go to the Cloisters.

- Liza is able to make Annie laugh — a good indication that Annie likes her. The joke isn't much — just that Liza hopes that Annie will not pose in front of a triptych or something.

The American Heritage® Dictionary of the English Language (Fourth Edition, 2000) defines "triptych" in this way: "A work consisting of three painted or carved panels that are hinged together."

What is the Cloisters?

The Cloisters is a museum of medieval art and architecture; it is a branch of the Metropolitan Museum of Art. It consists of a collection of buildings and of art. The buildings include a 12th-century Romanesque chapel, a chapter house, and some French cloisters. The art includes hundreds of examples of medieval painting and sculpture.

Dictionary.com gives these definitions of "cloister":

1. a covered walk, especially in a religious institution, having an open arcade or colonnade usually opening onto a courtyard.

2. a courtyard, especially in a religious institution, bordered with such walks.

3. a place of religious seclusion, as a monastery or convent.

4. any quiet, secluded place.

5. life in a monastery or convent.

Chapter 4

Write a character analysis of Ms. Widmer, the poetry teacher.

• She is a good teacher. She has a good voice for reading poetry, and she teaches well enough that her students also like poetry.

• She reads humorous poems, and she gives homework.

• She is a sympathetic character.

• She is not old, yet her hair is grey — something that she finds amusing.

• It is rumored that before graduation Ms. Widmer gives each graduating senior a poem that she thinks is relevant to their future life.

Why do you suppose author Nancy Garden put the poem "Invictus" in chapter 4? What does "invictus" mean?

William Ernest Henley (1849–1903) wrote "Invictus":

Invictus

Out of the night that covers me,
Black as the Pit from pole to pole,
I thank whatever gods may be
For my unconquerable soul.
In the fell clutch of circumstance 5
I have not winced nor cried aloud.
Under the bludgeonings of chance
My head is bloody, but unbowed.
Beyond this place of wrath and tears
Looms but the Horror of the shade, 10
And yet the menace of the years
Finds, and shall find, me unafraid.
It matters not how strait the gate,
How charged with punishments the scroll,
I am the master of my fate: 15
I am the captain of my soul.

• "Invictus" is Latin, and it means "unconquered" or "undefeated."

• The poem basically says that no matter what bad things are happening or will happen, the speaker's soul shall still be unconquered.

• Trivia: Oklahoma bomber Timothy McVeigh — a bad guy — copied out this poem shortly before he was executed.

• In this chapter, Liza is going through a bad time. However, she does not cave in, unlike Sally.

Write a character analysis of Angela Cariatid. What is a caryatid?

• Angela Cariatid is like a caryatid. She is tall and usually self-possessed. However, now she is not at all self possessed.

• Angela is very nervous, and she provides comic relief during the trial scene. For example, she hits the gavel so hard that it flies out of her hand.

• Although Angela is supposed to be running the disciplinary hearing, clearly Mrs. Poindexter is running it.

• *The Columbia Encyclopedia* (Sixth Edition, 2001) defines caryatid as "a sculptured female figure serving as an ornamental support in place of a column or pilaster." On the Acropolis in Athens, Greece, six caryatids make up part of the Porch of the Caryatids, which is part of the Erechtheum, an ancient Greek temple. By the way, male supporting figures also exist; they are called atlantes.

Did Mrs. Poindexter run the meeting in chapter 4 fairly? Why or why not?

• Although Angela is supposed to be running the disciplinary hearing, clearly Mrs. Poindexter is running it.

• Mrs. Poindexter says that Jennifer Piccolo volunteered to testify at the disciplinary hearing, but Liza suspects that Mrs. Poindexter volunteered Jennifer Piccolo to testify at the disciplinary hearing.

• Mrs. Poindexter points out the consequences of Sally's actions. It could really hurt the school's fundraising efforts.

• Mrs. Poindexter seems more worried about Jennifer's ears than other students' ears because Jennifer's father is on the fundraising committee.

• At one point, Mrs. Poindexter says to a student who has spoken up, "I did not see you raise your hand" (46). However, I don't think Mrs. Poindexter has been raising her hand when she wants to speak. Besides, Angela is the one who should be saying, "I did not see you raise your hand."

What does Ms. Stevenson do at the meeting?

• Ms. Stevenson is a sympathetic character again. She is opposed to Mrs. Poindexter's heavy-handedness.

• When Angela says that Sally and Liza broke the rules, Ms. Stevenson quietly points out that they are *accused* of breaking the rules.

• Ms. Stevenson points out that Sally did not ask Jennifer to get her ears pierced.

What is Sally's reaction to her trial and sentencing?

• Sally is not the captain of her soul. She is really overcome with guilt. She worries about Jennifer's ears.

• Liza writes, "I had never see Sally like this" (46).

What punishments do Liza and Sally receive?

• Both of them are suspended for a week. However, because of Thanksgiving, that is only a 3-day suspension.

• Liza will have to undergo a vote to determine of the student body have enough confidence in her for her to continue being the president of the student council. This vote regarding confidence or lack of it is Mrs. Poindexter's idea.

Chapter 5

Write a character analysis of Liza's father and mother based on what you learn in chapter 5. What do we learn about Liza's knowledge of her parents?

Liza

• We learn that Liza knows the best time to break bad news — such as news about her being suspended from school. That time is when her parents are relaxing with drinks before dinner.

Liza's Father

• We already knew that Liza's father is an engineer who graduated from MIT. Now we learn that he is a perfectionist. He wants his children to be perfect. He thinks that Liza should have acted in a more mature way than she did when she discovered that Sally was piercing ears.

• Liza's father doesn't think much about Sally. We get the idea that he thinks that she is a kind of airhead.

Liza's Mother

• Liza's mother sticks up for all the members of her family: her husband, daughter, and son. Here, she defends Liza by saying that she is still an adolescent and so can't be expected to be perfect.

• Liza's mother also points out that the school is coming down harder on Liza than on Sally (something that Liza's mother doesn't think is fair) — but that is in part because Liza is in a leadership position.

How does Liza and Annie's relationship advance in chapter 5?

• At first, they are tongue-tied when they get together to go to the Cloisters.

• They do find something to talk about, of course — Liza tells Annie about the ear-piercing incident. Annie is on Liza's side.

• Annie strikes (52) a religious pose that Liza has seen in a hundred medieval paintings. This shows that both Liza and Annie are interested in art and in learning.

• Annie enjoys play-acting — this time she pretends to be a medieval damsel (52) — since the Cloisters is supposed to be a medieval monastery, that is appropriate. This time, Liza pretends to be her knight. This time, Liza is not as self-conscious as she was previously, although many more people are present than were present in the Metropolitan Museum of Art.

• The two learn more about each other. Annie's school is much different from Liza's. Annie's school has many more security personnel around, and the problems don't involve ear piercings but instead things like assault and possession of illegal drugs.

• The two learn more about each other. Annie has pierced ears, and Liza doesn't want pierced ears.

• Annie seems more creative than Liza. Annie enjoys play-acting, and sometimes Liza has to struggle to keep up with her. Annie can imitate a lion with a human mustache, and she can imitate a unicorn.

• Liza and Annie seem to think the same thoughts. They are both sad that the caged unicorn in the unicorn tapestries looks so sad.

• They have a picnic — Annie has brought the food. At the picnic, the two continue to pretend that they are living in medieval times. Annie, of course, takes the lead, but Liza willingly follows. Annie admits that most people don't do this sort of pretending after they are older than seven.

• Annie would like wine at the picnic, but she has brought coffee. (People don't always believe that she is old enough to buy wine — after all, she is only 17.)

• Liza acted out King Arthur stories until she was 14, but she still thinks about the stories.

• Annie's family's name was not originally Kenyon, but something long and complicated in Italian.

• We find out Annie wants to go to college — her grades are good, especially in music. She also has a Nana — an Italian grandmother. Her mother is a hard-working bookkeeper — supposedly part-time, but she works late a lot. Her first choice for a college is Berkeley.

• The conversation between Liza and Annie flows freely — as if they are following a script.

• Annie thinks that Liza is the first friendly person she has met since she moved to New York — Annie used to live in San José, California.

Who is Sir Thomas Malory and what is the *Morte d'Arthur*?

Sir Thomas Malory (d. 1471), an English knight, wrote the *Morte d'Arthur*, a collection of tales (romances) about King Arthur, Camelot, and the Knights of the Round Table. Actually, Sir Thomas titled his book *The Book of King Arthur and His Noble Knights of the Round Table*, but in 1485 William Caxton (who introduced printing into England) printed the book and gave it the title *Morte d'Arthur*, which means *The Death of Arthur*. The *Morte d'Arthur* includes the knights' quest for the Holy Grail, which is usually thought to be the goblet from which Jesus drank at the Last Supper.

According to *The Columbia Encyclopedia* (Sixth Edition, 2008):

> The *Morte d'Arthur* is noted for its excellent dramatic narrative and the beauty of its rhythmic and simple language. It remains the standard source for later versions of the legend.

If you feel like doing research, identify the Unicorn Tapestries that Liza and Annie look at.

The Unicorn Tapestries are on display at the Cloisters. They consist of seven hangings. These beautiful hangings are believed to date from 1495–1505. They may have been woven in Brussels after having been designed in Paris. Often, the Unicorn Tapestries are referred to as "The Hunt of the Unicorn."

John D. Rockefeller bought and kept the Unicorn Tapestries until 1937, and then he gave them to the Cloisters. He also gave much other medieval art to the Cloisters.

How does Liza and Annie's relationship advance when they meet again later in chapter 5?

• The two meet again on a Sunday when Liza is in a bad mood. It seems like every topic of conversation has to do with earrings or with teenagers getting in trouble, so she goes for a walk. During the walk, she meets Annie.

• Annie had come to see where Liza lives. Finding that Liza was out, Annie was able to get information from Liza's mother and Chad, Liza's brother, about where Liza probably was.

• Annie does give good advice — which comes originally from Nana, her mountain-climbing grandmother. Nana says that climbing mountains is tough, but that there's a worthwhile view at the top of each mountain. Being president of student council is tough — because everyone expects you to be perfect — but the view from the top (the reward) is worth it. Annie also tells Liza not to be perfect for other people.

• The two are speaking as if they have known each other for years instead of just a few days. They are able to be serious together, and they are able to be frivolous together.

• Liza's mom invites Annie to supper. (Liza's mom is very nice.)

• Annie and Liza's mom get along so well that Liza feels shut out of their conversation — which is about Bach and Brahms and Schubert (63) — that Liza has to hint for the subject of conversation to be changed to one that she can participate more in. Liza's mom is intelligent as well as nice — she gets the hint quickly and changes the topic of conversation.

• Annie gets to see Liza's room, which is a mess. Liza has a drawing table in her room. Annie seems genuinely interested in architecture, but when Liza tries later to make conversation about music, Annie says that Liza doesn't have make conversation about something that she is not really interested in. They really do seem compatible with each other.

- Liza, her Dad, and Chad all ride with Annie on the subway back to her home. This shows how nice Liza and her family are.

- Annie is a little embarrassed about where she lives. She lives in a much less nice neighborhood than Liza and her family. Liza's dad insists on taking Annie to her apartment out of concern for her safety. Annie's neighborhood has beggars in it.

- Liza's dad can be humorous — he jokes about Liza being in an ear-piercing ring — and he does tell Liza that everyone makes mistakes.

What do you think about the ending of Chapter 5?

- This ending is designed to pique the reader's interest and keep the reader reading:

> But, oh, God, neither of us had any way of knowing that I would do something much, much worse [than not stopping Sally from piercing ears] — at least in the eyes of the school and my parents, and probably a whole lot of other people, too, if they had known about it. (66)

Interlude

What happens during this short interlude?
- We learn that Liza likes classical music.
- We learn that Liza is still thinking about Annie, although she would like to avoid that. In fact, she takes a couple of long walks, puts in three hours of unnecessary lab work, and goes to the library to avoid thinking about Annie — but ends up thinking about her anyway.
- We note that all of Annie's letters except the last one has said, "I miss you" (67).
- Liza does have Annie's photograph.

Chapter 6

Write a character analysis of Ms. Widmer and Ms. Stevenson based on what you learn in chapter 6. (Ms. Widmer and Ms. Stevenson will be important characters later.)

- We find out that Ms. Widmer and Ms. Stevenson live together.
- We find out that they are close. Ms. Widmer is late for school because she is talking care of Isabelle — she then refers to her quickly as "Ms. Stevenson" because she is talking to Liza on the telephone. (Liza has called to find out about her homework while she is suspended.)
- Ms. Stevenson is a good teacher. She wants Liza to keep up with her schoolwork while she is suspended.

How does Annie and Liza's relationship advance in chapter 6?

- The two continue to get to know each other better. Liza visits Annie at her school, and they take the ferry back and forth to Staten Island.
- Annie knows that there is somewhere better than where she is now. This conversation shows that the two can really talk about important things. Annie remembers seeing white birds (actually white houses) in San Francisco — that is a better place than where she is right now.
- Annie reads a lot, although her school teaches little or no history. That is how she is able to pretend so well.
- They do some more pretending (this time, pretending to travel to somewhere than where they really are traveling), but Annie says that she wants to be real with Liza.
- The two girls are observant — they laugh at a woman (Mommy) and her dog.
- The two girls are touching a little more. As they walk, their shoulders touch. They don't move apart because it would be an acknowledgement that they are touching. The two also hold hands.

• Liza calls Annie "fascinating" (76), and Annie says the same thing about Liza (77).

Chapters 6-7

Compare and contrast Annie's school and Liza's school.

Annie's School

Ch. 6

• Annie's school is like a prison. It has a number of security officers, and apparently a lot of crime happens there.

• Liza is unable to get into the school after she admits that she was suspended from her own school. When Liza and Annie meet, Annie apologizes, saying that she should have warned Liza more about the security officers. Annie also says that the security officers probably thought that Liza was a drug dealer.

• Liza ends up spending time at another museum — the Museum of the American Indian — before meeting Annie.

Ch. 7

• A kid in the cafeteria pulls out a length of chain and starts twirling it. The other kids ignore him, but a carpentry teacher comes along and takes the chain from the kid. Annie tells us that the boy does that roughly every week. We get the idea that the kid is mentally ill and that no one is getting him the help he needs.

• Annie used to cry — for a couple of months — because she was attending this school. Then she got used to it. She continues to attend this school instead of another one so that she can look in on her grandmother during lunchtime. That way, she will know that her grandmother is OK.

• Annie discovered that if she left the other kids alone, that they would leave her alone. That is why she doesn't have any friends there. By the time she discovered who the normal kids were, they had already made other friends. Thus Annie is alone.

Liza's School

• Liza's school, of course, is private, not public.

• Liza's school doesn't need all the security that Annie's school has.

• Liza's school may have deal with the problem of infected ears from ear piercing, but it apparently doesn't have to worry about assaults and illegal drugs.

Chapter 7

Write a character analysis of Nana based on what you learn in chapter 7.

- Nana is Annie's grandmother. She is tiny, and she is in a wheelchair.
- She has bright blue eyes and a puckered mouth that smiles the way that Annie smiles.
- She is at home alone while Annie is in school and Annie's mother is working.
- Nana was born in Italy.
- Nana identifies the gift that Liza has brought for Annie: an African violet. Annie loves flowers, as Liza knows from a trip they make together to the New York Botanical Garden.
- Annie's family is making the turkey the day before Thanksgiving so that they can relax on Thanksgiving.
- Nana likes Liza because she makes Annie happy — Annie is sometimes sad.
- Nana is religious — the cross on the wall (and the palm leaf) is hers.
- Annie says that Nana adores Liza.
- Until Nana's fingers grew too arthritic, she made all of Annie's clothes

Compare and contrast Annie's apartment and room and Liza's apartment and room.

- The buzzer of Annie's apartment doesn't work.
- Annie's apartment is dingy compared to Liza's. The couch has some stuffing coming out, and the carpet once was bright red — a long time ago.
- Annie's room has a narrow bed, one chair, and a table that serves as a desk.

• The table is covered with music scores and books, so we know that Annie is creative and intelligent. (We have already seen evidence that Annie actually studies the music scores and books.)

• Annie's bedroom has many stuffed animals and many plants. The furniture is worn, and a hole in a broken window has been stuffed with a rag to keep out drafts.

• Earlier, we learned that Liza's bedroom was sloppy. Annie talks about Liza's room — it is shiny and new.

• Liza says that she likes Annie's room, Nana — and Annie. Annie replies that she like Liza.

• Lots of cats are in Annie's apartment.

• Annie is a good hostess, as is her family. Annie and Liza drink grape juice and eat Italian cookies. When Liza leaves, she takes Italian cookies home for Chad.

What do we learn about Annie in chapter 7?

• Annie has some insecurities. She cries because Liza bought her a present, and she doesn't have the money to reciprocate.

• Annie had a friend in the 6th grade, and she was very upset when the friend moved away.

• At night, Annie sometimes listens to Nana breathe. Annie is afraid that Nana will die.

• Annie is sometimes embarrassed by her family.

How does Annie and Liza's relationship advance on Thanksgiving and the following Sunday?

Thanksgiving

• The families get to know each other a little.

• Annie's Dad is a cab driver. They take Nana for a ride on holidays. Annie's Dad wonders if Liza's family wants to go for a cab ride. That way, the two families can get to know each other. This embarrasses Annie; however, Liza tells us that she likes Annie's family. Annie's Dad is an immigrant — he has been in the United States since he was 20.

• Annie does love her family — although she doesn't like her school or her neighborhood.

• Liza does get angry for a moment — she wonders if Annie envies her. (A kind of reverse slumming.)

• Only Liza takes the cab ride. However, the other members of her family do meet the Kenyons.

• Liza likes Mr. Kenyon a lot. Mr. Kenyon's father had been a butcher in Italy, and cats used to follow him around. The Kenyons still have cats because a home does not seem to be a home without a few cats around.

• Mr. Kenyon and Nana tell lots of stories about Italy.

The Following Sunday

• Liza and Annie go to Coney Island.

• They are sad because they won't be able to meet as easily and as often. School is starting. Annie has to practice for her music recital. Liza will probably be busy with Student Council, and she has a senior project to do.

• It's chilly, Liza puts her arm across Annie's shoulders to warm up, and they start kissing.

• Neither is exactly sure what to do. Annie says that it is OK with her if it OK with Liza, but Liza doesn't know what to think.

• One part of Liza says that this is wrong, but another part says that it is exactly right.

• Annie has wondered if the two were falling in love.

• On p. 94, we see the word "gay" used for the first time, and Liza says to Annie that she thinks she loves her. As soon as she says it, she knows that it is true.

Interlude

What happens during this short interlude?

- Once again, we are in the present time.
- Once again, Liza is thinking about Annie.
- Liza has been writing a letter to Annie, but she ends up tearing it up.

Chapter 8

Write a character analysis of Sally Jarrell.

- Sally Jarrell is in danger of becoming a conformist.

- She feels really guilty about the ear-piercing incident, and so apologizes to the entire student body and volunteers for the student part of the fund-raising effort

- She snaps at Liza when Liza doesn't know how much she will contribute to the fund-raising effort. However, Sally then immediately apologizes.

- Sally is not a totally evil character, but she is being influenced by Ms. Baxter.

- In Sally, we see a nonconformist becoming a conformist. We also see a free spirit becoming unduly influenced by adult authority.

How does Annie and Liza's relationship advance in chapter 8?

- Liza does get to continue to be president of Student Council. But because things seem weird at her school (Sally seems weird), she calls Annie. She then visits her.

- Sunday is hanging over this meeting between Liza and Annie. They remember kissing each other. They hug when they get to Annie's room, but Liza pulls away.

- Annie has written Liza a letter. Annie is pretty sure that she is gay. That is one reason she told Liza about her previous best friend, Beverly. Annie tried to show that she is not gay with a boy last summer, but that effort was "ridiculous" (104).

- Liza is confused. She knows that there are some things in her life that suggest that she is gay:

  - Even when she was young, she felt as if she did not fit it.

  - She prefers to go to the movies with another girl than with a boy.

• When she thinks about settling down with someone, that someone is always female.

• She loves Annie.

• Liza does not want to tear up the letter, although in it Annie said that it would be OK if Liza did not want to see her again. This is the first letter that Annie has written to her, and Liza wants to keep it.

• Liza and Annie end up in bed, kissing occasionally but mostly feeling happy rather than touching. (Liza still feels scared, though.)

Chapter 9

How does Annie and Liza's relationship advance in chapter 9?

• This chapter is all about their relationship. One part of the relationship that is NOT happening is the physical, sexual part. This is partly because they are afraid, partly because they don't want the same thing at the same time, and partly because they don't have a place where they can be alone.

Closeness

• They see each other often, and they call each other often.

• Obviously, they are in love. Liza thinks more about Annie than about her schoolwork.

• Liza buys Annie lots of plants — she would buy more if she didn't know that Annie is bothered because she can't reciprocate with gifts. (Annie does not have as much money as Liza.)

• They share things with each other — often, things about New York. For example, the sunlight on Annie's ugly apartment building at times softens it and makes it glow. And ailanthus trees grow under subway and sewer gratings.

First Date

• It is Annie's idea that they have a dinner date. And this is a real date. Heterosexuals have dates for dinner, so Annie and Liza think that they should, too.

• The date happens in an Italian restaurant.

• They have such a good time and stay so long that both sets of parents are mad at them when they finally get home.

• Liza's dad wants Liza to see more people than just Annie.

Touching

• Liza and Annie touch more easily now — they are hugging and kissing.

• Chad thinks that Liza is in love with a boy. A couple of people at school — Sally and Walt — begin to think the same thing.

Snowballs

• The two share a lot. For example, when there is a snowfall, they call each other on the telephone for 10 minutes. They always get a busy signal because each is calling the other. Finally, the two get connected to each other and arrange to go to Central Park, where they throw snowballs and have fun.

• They also go ice skating a few times.

Christmas Presents

• Each gets the other a Christmas present.

• Each gets the other a gold ring with a stone.

• The rings are very similar, but are not identical. One stone is pale green; the other stone is pale blue.

• Annie tells Liza, *"Buon Natale, amore mio"* (112). Liza tells Annie, "Merry Christmas, my love" (112).

Annie's Recital

• Annie has talent.

• Annie is a mezzo-soprano.

• Liza's mother knows something about music, and she talks to Annie about singing professionally. Annie wants to continue singing and to study music in college, but she doesn't know about trying to sing professionally.

The Flu

• Liza gets the flu, and Annie tells Liza's mother that she has already had the flu that year so she can visit Liza and comfort her. (Annie actually had the flu the previous year.)

• Annie sings to Liza to comfort her.

Stirrings of Sexual Feelings

• The two want to touch, but they avoid it. This affects their relationship.

• They are in Annie's room. Annie's hands begin to wander, and she touches Liza's breast. Liza adjusts the radio dial.

• They touch while doing the dishes at Liza's. Liza holds Annie from behind, but when Annie turns toward her, Liza grabs a towel and begins to dry some dishes.

• In the subway, Liza kisses Annie (they are alone), and Annie turns away.

The Fight

• The lack of sexual satisfaction leads to fights. The fights are over minor things, such as what time they will meet and what they will do. The biggest fight occurs at the Metropolitan Museum of Art. Should they continue to look at the Unicorn Tapestries or go to the Temple of Dendur?

• They fight, and Liza calls Annie to apologize, but Annie is already in bed. Liza asks Nana to tell Annie that she is sorry.

Stirrings of Sexual Feelings

• Neither sleeps well that night, and Annie shows up at Liza's house the next day after school.

• Annie is worried that Liza thinks that physical love — sex — is dirty. Annie is willing to do without sex with Liza as long as she can be with Liza.

• Liza realizes that she wants physical love with Annie.

• One major problem that they face is that it is so difficult for them to be alone together. Once, they are on the couch when Liza's dad comes home. Fortunately, they hear his key turning in the lock. (Even when they are alone in one of their apartments, they are afraid that someone will walk in on them.)

• Another factor is that Liza thinks that they simply need more time.

Retell the myth by Plato that explains why humans are sometimes heterosexual and sometimes homosexual. (The character named Aristophanes tells this myth in Plato's *Symposium*.)

• This myth appears in Plato's *Symposium*. Its speaker is Aristophanes, a writer of comic plays.

• At one time, three genders exist: male, female, and a combination of the two (androgynous).

• The three genders were proud, and they attacked the gods.

• To punish the three genders, Zeus and the other gods split them into two parts.

• The halves desire to be reunited, so they search for each other. The halves of the male gender seek each other; they are homosexual men, aka gay men. The halves of the female gender seek each other; they are homosexual women, aka lesbians. The halves of the androgynous gender seek each other; they are heterosexual men and women.

Chapter 10

What do we learn about Mrs. Poindexter and Ms. Baxter in chapter 10?

• Mrs. Poindexter is still pushy. She arranges for a meeting of Student Council without first asking — or even telling — Liza. She also asks Ms. Widmer and Ms. Stevenson to "volunteer" their house for the meeting. The purpose of the meeting is to get Student Council more involved in the fund-raising campaign.

• Ms. Poindexter even calls Liza "dear" (125) when she says that Foster Academy may be forced to close.

• Mrs. Poindexter loves Foster Academy, and she is genuinely worried about whether it can financially survive.

• Ms. Baxter is still Mrs. Poindexter's toady. She does the dirty work of asking Ms. Stevenson — the Student Council advisor — to "volunteer" her house.

• Ms. Baxter takes notes at the meeting, which makes Mary Lou (the Student Council Treasurer) "furious" (132).

• Of course, Mrs. Poindexter tries to run the meeting.

• Both Mrs. Poindexter and Ms. Baxter seem rather snobbish. They seem to think that Foster Academy and its students are better than other schools and other students. Liza and others point out that Foster Academy has a snobbish reputation.

• Liza feels that although the public schools have more problems than other schools, that they are nevertheless more interesting — by which she probably means that they are more interesting because they are more diverse.

• Ms. Baxter is really worried about morality. She wants everyone to be on their best behavior so that a scandal will not threaten the school's fund-raising effort.

• At the end of the chapter, Mrs. Poindexter and Ms. Baxter sing the silly school song. They are old women who seem to wish that they were 15 years old again.

What do we learn about Ms. Widmer and Ms. Stevenson in chapter 10?

• Ms. Stevenson "volunteers" her and Ms. Widmer's house, although she isn't happy about it. She puts on a happy face for Liza, but Liza sees in the wastebasket a number of pieces of paper covered with angry-looking writing.

• Ms. Stevenson, however, recognizes that Mrs. Poindexter genuinely cares about Foster Academy.

• Liza is the first to arrive, and she is shown the bottom two stories of the row house. (The third story is where the bedrooms are.)

• Ms. Widmer and Ms. Stevenson seem to have lived together a long time. There are very comfortable with each other. Everything in the apartment appears to be jointly owned. It's not as if they are saying, "This is my armchair; this is your couch."

• Their house has three floors:

   • Bottom: Kitchen and Dining Room and Small Bathroom (outside, a garden area)

   • Middle: Living Room and Study

   • Top: Apparently, Two Bedrooms

• Liza learns that Ms. Stevenson smokes, which surprises her. (What surprises me is that students at Foster Academy can smoke in the Senior Lounge.) Ms. Stevenson once tried to quit, but she gained a lot of weight and was so irritable that she decided to start smoking again.

What foreshadowing do we have in chapter 10?

• There is foreshadowing in that Ms. Widmer and Ms. Stevenson have cats. They are going away on vacation, and the boy who looks after the cats is going away on vacation, and so they are wondering who will take care of the cats.

• Liza volunteers to take care of the cats. She is willing to accept as pay whatever the boy who took care of the cats was paid: $1.50 per day.

• Later, we will see that Liza gets the key to the apartment, and that is where Liza and Annie will be able to be alone.

Chapter 11

How does Annie and Liza's relationship advance in chapter 11?

• Both girls get good news. They have both been accepted by colleges. Unfortunately, they are on different coasts. MIT is on the east coast, and Berkeley is on the west coast.

• In addition, both girls know that they will be separated for most of the summer. Annie will be a counselor at a music camp in California.

• Liza and her family attend Annie's recital. Of course, Annie sings a song especially for Liza. (Of course, she doesn't announce publicly that that is what she is doing.)

• Liza and Annie spend some time together, and sometimes they hold hands in public — when it is unlikely that anyone they know will see them.

• The two girls go to the Japanese Garden at the Botanic Garden. It is the best time to be there — spring, when most of the trees are in bloom.

• Liza wants more information on homosexuality — she realizes that she is in love with Annie and is therefore a homosexual. She looks up "homosexuality" in an encyclopedia — and she is angered because the entry doesn't once mention the word "love."

• Annie tells Liza that encyclopedias are not a good source of information for what Liza wants to know. Apparently, Annie has already read a few encyclopedia entries. Instead, she recommends a novel titled *Patience and Sarah*, by Isabel Miller.

• Liza and Annie buy a couple of gay newspapers and magazines. Buying this material terrifies them, but Liza sees part of herself in the gay people she reads about.

• At the end of the chapter, Annie and Liza realize that they do have a place where they can be alone together — the row house of Ms. Widmer and Ms. Stevenson. (Obviously, this is a good way to end a chapter — the reader will want to know what happens next.)

If you feel like doing research, find out about the book *Patience and Sarah* and report on what you discover. (Go to http://www.patienceandsarah.com.)

• Alma Routsong wrote the lesbian novel *Patience and Sarah*, a story about two women in love: Patience White and Sarah Dowling. The novel is set in 1816 in New England, which at the time is puritanical and hostile to homosexuals. In the novel, the two women take turns narrating the action.

Chapter 12

How does Annie and Liza's relationship advance in chapter 12?

• Their relationship advances quite a bit in this chapter. For one thing, they have a place where they can be alone and private together, and they take advantage of that.

• A lot of what they do is simply hang out together, as if this were their own house or apartment. They make coffee and bring food, so that they can spend the day together there. (They do go home to eat the evening meal with their family.)

• About her first time being physical with Annie, Liza writes:

I can close my eyes and feel every motion of Annie's body and my own — clumsy and hesitant and shy — but that isn't the important part. The important part is the wonder of the closeness and the unbearable ultimate realization that are two people, not one — and also the wonder of that: that even though we *are* two people, we can be almost like one, and at the same time delight in each other's uniqueness. (146)

• Liza writes that sometimes she and Annie had to stop what they were doing and simply "hold each other — too much beauty can be hard to bear" (150).

• However, they do get physical. They don't know much about what are doing at first, but they learn as they go. At first, they are somewhat shy with each other, but they grow more comfortable together.

• There is a brief scene in which a heavyset woman asks who they are when they are in the garden. They explain that the boy who usually takes care of the cats when Ms. Widmer and Ms. Stevenson are on vacation is on vacation himself, and so they are taking care of the cats.

The woman relaxes then and talks to them for an hour. It is a way to get out of the housework, although she doesn't seem to mind her life as a stay-at-home housewife (despite complaining a little).

- Note that Liza and Annie do respect Ms. Widmer and Ms. Stevenson's privacy. They haven't (yet) been to the third floor where the bedrooms are, and Annie decides not to work in their garden in case it would bother them.

Chapter 13

What do Annie and Liza discover when they go up to the third floor?

• They end up on the third floor because they can't find one of the cats. (The cat is on the third floor.)

• The main thing that they discover is that Ms. Widmer and Ms. Stevenson are gay.

• Ms. Widmer and Ms. Stevenson have a secret bookcase filled with gay books, including *Patience and Sarah*.

• In one bedroom is a double bed, which is used. In the other bedroom is a bed that is basically for show.

• In one bedroom are most of their clothes; in the other bedroom are seldom used articles of clothing.

Compare and contrast Annie and Liza's relationship with Ms. Widmer and Ms. Stevenson's relationship.

• Ms. Widmer and Ms. Stevenson are closeted, and they have been for a long time. However, later we will see a reason for their being closeted.

• Liza and Annie want to have an open relationship, although they don't think that they can have one now. They would like to not hide their relationship, but Annie doesn't want to tell Nana, and Liza doesn't want to tell her parents.

• Of course, Ms. Widmer and Ms. Stevenson are a long-established gay couple, whereas Annie and Liza are a new gay couple.

• We definitely see a difference between the different-aged couples. Ms. Widmer and Ms. Stevenson perhaps have settled into a sex-less relationship (Annie and Liza seem to think that they have, although Ms. Widmer and Ms. Stevenson may have a very different opinion). Liza and Annie, however, want to get it on.

If you feel like doing research, find and read one or more coming-out stories (stories in which a homosexual reveals that he

or she is gay). **What is your reaction to the story or stories you have researched?**

Here are two good sources to use:

https://whenicameout.com
http://www.bibble.org/gay/stories/comingout.html

What do you think of the way chapter 13 ends?

• Liza and Annie don't mean to end up in bed together, but they do. They are ignoring physicality on the conscious level and are instead playing childish games. They end up on the third floor, and the bed is just too tempting for them.

• Liza and Annie are in bed, being physical, when they hear the front door handle rattle.

• Obviously, the reader will want to know what will happen next.

• This is an excellent way to end this chapter.

Interlude

What happens during this short interlude?

- Once again, we are in the present time.
- Liza is writing a letter to Annie, but she is not sure that she will mail it.
- Liza is hung up on wondering whether homosexuality hurts no one. Perhaps she is thinking that it can hurt someone.
- The interlude keeps us reading. As always, we want to know what will happen with Liza and Annie's relationship.
- Liza's letter mentions gay animals. Read the book review at

    http://www.salon.com/it/feature/1999/03/
    cov_15featurea.html

and see what you learn.

- Here are two paragraphs from Susan McCarthy's book review of Bruce Bagemihl's *Biological Exuberance: Animal Homosexuality and Natural Diversity*:

They've been keeping it from us: There are homosexual and bisexual animals, ranging from charismatic megafauna like mountain gorillas to cats, dogs and guinea pigs. There are transgendered animals, transvestite animals (who adopt the behavior of the other gender but don't have sex with their own), and animals who live in bisexual triads and quartets.

Bruce Bagemihl spent 10 years scouring the biological literature for data on alternative sexuality in animals to write *Biological Exuberance: Animal Homosexuality and Natural Diversity*, 768 pages about exactly what goes on at *South Park*'s Big Gay Al's Big Gay Animal Sanctuary. The first section discusses animal sexuality in its many forms and the ways biologists have tried to explain it away. The second section, "A Wondrous Bestiary," describes unconventional sexuality in nearly 200 mammals and birds — orangutans, whales, warthogs, fruit bats, chaffinches.

Source: Susan McCarthy, "The FABULOUS kingdom of GAY animals." Salon.com. 1999
http://www.salon.com/1999/03/16/cov_15featurea

Chapter 14

What is Ms. Baxter's reaction to Annie and Liza's relationship and to Ms. Widmer and Ms. Stevenson's relationship? What is Sally's reaction?

• Both Ms. Baxter and Sally have a bad reaction to both lesbian relationships.

• Sally immediately guesses that Annie and Liza are gay. Annie and Liza are partially dressed, and she sees them being uncomfortable and also holding hands. Sally seems uncomfortable with this lesbian relationship.

• Ms. Baxter is religious, and she is very much against homosexuality. We find out that she has long suspected that Ms. Widmer and Ms. Stevenson were gay, but that she held her tongue. For one thing, she lacked proof. For another, Ms. Widmer and Ms. Stevenson hid their homosexuality, so Ms. Baxter thought that it would have no ill effect on the students. However, since Liza is in a gay relationship, apparently it has had a bad relationship on the students — so Ms. Baxter thinks.

• Ms. Baxter becomes aware that Ms. Widmer and Ms. Stevenson are gay because of their reading matter. (She won't call it literature.) This is the same thing that convinced Annie and Liza that Ms. Widmer and Ms. Stevenson were gay.

• Ms. Baxter thinks that she needs to protect Sally from lesbians.

• Ms. Baxter seems to believe that Ms. Widmer and Ms. Stevenson deliberately let Annie and Liza use their house as a place to have lesbian sex.

• Ms. Baxter will immediately inform Mrs. Poindexter that Ms. Widmer and Ms. Stevenson are lesbians.

What does *in flagrante delicto* mean?

• The phrase *in flagrante delicto* is Latin for "in the commission of the act." The phrase is used to refer to people who are caught having sex together.

• Note that Liza does not think that what she and Annie were doing is ugly.

Ms. Baxter thinks that the situation in Ms. Widmer and Mr. Stevenson's house is similar to Sodom and Gomorrah. If you feel like doing research, explain what are Sodom and Gomorrah.

Sodom and Gomorrah are cities whose citizens were known for their sinfulness. Because of this, God destroyed both cities.

From the name "Sodom," we get the word "sodomy."

The New Dictionary of Cultural Literacy, Third Edition, defines Sodomy in this way:

> Sexual intercourse that is not the union of the genital organs of a man and a woman. The term is most frequently applied to anal intercourse between two men or to sexual relations between people and animals.

After I show my students at Ohio University this definition on a transparency, I ask them this: "How many of you are going to telephone your mother tonight and say, 'Hey, Mom, guess what I learned in school today?'"

How do Ms. Widmer and Ms. Stevenson react when they come home?

• Ms. Stevenson nearly drops her suitcase. Ms. Widmer does drop her suitcase.

• Both are angry at Ms. Baxter. She can seriously harm their lives. She can get them fired.

• Both regard what Liza has done as a "rather serious betrayal of trust" (171).

• Ms. Stevenson has to fight back tears after Ms. Baxter and Sally have gone.

• Ms. Widmer is more understanding. Liza is 17. Can she really control her desires?

• They are still nice people. They make cocoa, and they allow 15 minutes for Annie and Liza to get dressed and for everyone to collect and calm themselves. (Ms. Stevenson needs — and gets — Scotch, not cocoa.)

Chapter 15

How do Ms. Widmer and Ms. Stevenson treat Liza and Annie?

• Much better than the night before. With Ms. Widmer's help, Ms. Stevenson remembers what it is like to be 17, gay, and in love. She admits that if she and Ms. Widmer had had a house available to them when they were 17, they may not have controlled themselves either. (We find out that they actually have known each other since they were 17; theirs is a long-term and long-lasting relationship.)

• Little real conversation occurs, although things start out well with Liza and Annie explaining about the saucepan helmets.

• Basically, everyone is too worried about what will happen that they can't actually converse well. However, Ms. Widmer and Ms. Stevenson tell Liza that she will have to tell her parents — they will find out. Rumors will be swirling around school. Annie doesn't attend Liza's school, so she is still safe.

Why won't Annie tell her family that she is gay? Does she have a good reason?

• Annie basically gives three reasons for not telling her family, although another reason could be that she isn't forced to tell her family, the way that Liza is:

1) Annie says that she won't tell her family that she is gay because it would hurt them.

2) Annie says that she won't tell her family that she is gay because it is not part of their world.

3) Annie says that she won't tell her family that she is gay because she isn't sure that she is gay.

• The third reason is poor. Annie says it because Liza says that she isn't sure that she is gay. Of course, Liza does admit both to herself and to Annie that she is gay and that Annie is her lover.

• The other reasons are better, but who knows how her family will react? Some parents (and grandmothers) react very well; others don't.

• Of course, we remember that earlier that Annie said that she didn't want to live a closeted life.

What is Mrs. Poindexter's reaction to Annie and Liza's relationship?

• Mrs. Poindexter regards the relationship of Liza and Annie as an unnatural relationship. (So, apparently, does Ms. Baxter, who prays when Annie is near her in this chapter.)

• Mrs. Poindexter does recognize that the sex drive can be strong when one is 17. She says that she and her husband might have committed a mistake when they were 17 if not for their strong religious upbringing. (Liza has to force herself not to smile at the thought of Mrs. Poindexter — now a widow — having at one time been passionate.)

• Mrs. Poindexter thinks that Ms. Widmer and Ms. Stevenson may have encouraged Liza and Annie to have sex in their house.

• Mrs. Poindexter is really shocked by what Liza and Annie have done — apparently, she has been crying.

• Mrs. Poindexter is especially worried about the fund-raising effort to save Foster Academy.

• Mrs. Poindexter calls Liza's parents to tell them what has happened. (Liza did not tell her parents the night before. Chad was around, and she didn't want to tell them in front of Chad.) In addition, when there was a chance to tell them when they were going to bed, she decided to wait another day and see what Mrs. Poindexter would do.)

• Lisa is suspended from school. She is no longer a part of the fund-raising effort. She can no longer be President of Student Council.

- Ms. Poindexter even speaks of alerting MIT to Liza's "proclivities" (184).
- There will be a kind of "trial" for Liza.

What happens in the interlude within chapter 15?

- Liza is wondering about helping others and about immorality in this interlude within chapter 15.
- Does helping others involve helping people to be like other people or helping people to be themselves? Gays don't want to be like other people. They want to be themselves.
- Does immorality mainly involve hurting people? Does being homosexual really hurt other people?

What are Liza's parents' reactions to what they know about Annie and Liza's relationship?

- Liza takes her time getting home because she wants to put off seeing her Mom.
- When Liza does get home, she discovered that her Mom has been crying.
- Liza's mom does her best to comfort Liza, but she thinks that Liza's lesbian relationship has been a kind of experiment, that her sexual feelings are confused, that she isn't a lesbian really.
- Liza has to leave or blurt out angry words. Liza thinks that her relationship with Annie is a beautiful and wonderful thing.
- Liza does lie to her mother. She says that she and Annie have just been experimenting — nothing more. Liza's mother is immensely relieved, but all Liza can think is that she has lied to her mother for the first time.
- When Liza's dad comes in, his face is gray. He does say that he will support Liza. No matter what, she is his daughter.
- We remember that Liza's dad doesn't like it when other people make racist or homophobic jokes.
- Liza's dad doesn't care if Ms. Widmer and Ms. Stevenson are lesbians. The important thing is that they are good teachers.

• Liza's mom immediately accepted Liza's lie that she and Annie had simply experimented. Her dad is much more skeptical.

• Liza's dad tells her that he has always thought that homosexuals can't be happy. Liza feels that she can be happy with Annie and with work as an architect — but she doesn't say anything out loud.

• Liza's mom takes her shopping. The excuse is that they might as well buy Liza's MIT clothes, but the real reason is that her Dad wants to talk alone with Chad when school lets out.

What happens to Ms. Widmer and Ms. Stevenson?

• Ms. Widmer and Ms. Stevenson are suspended.

What are the reactions of Liza's fellow students to what they know about Annie and Liza's relationship?

• Walt grins at her. Liza thinks the grin is a little strange at first.

• A couple of other students look at her funny.

• When Liza opens her locker to clean it out, she finds a note: "LIZA LESIE."

• When Liza calls Sally later, Sally hangs up.

• When Liza meets Sally later to give Sally her notes for the fund-raising speech, Sally is wondering how Liza could have sex with a girl. Sally is shocked, not curious.

Read Leviticus 18:22. What is your reaction?

• The King James translation of Leviticus 18:22 is this:

Thou shalt not lie with mankind, as with womankind: it is abomination.

• One thing to note is that this verse says nothing about same-sex sexual relationships between two women.

• A good source to consult is

http://www.religioustolerance.org/hom_bibh.htm

This source points out the difficulty of translating and interpreting this passage.

• Another good source to consult is this:

Helminiak, Daniel A. *What the Bible Really Says About Homosexuality*. San Francisco, CA: Alamo Square Press, c1994. Foreword by John S. Spong.

• On June 23, 2008, I downloaded this information from http://www.religioustolerance.org/hom_bibh5.htm:

Some liberal Christian Interpretations:

Some English translations of this passage condemn both gay and lesbian sexual relationships. This is a mistranslation. It refers only to male-male sexual behavior.

This passage does not refer to gay sex generally, but only to a specific form of homosexual prostitution in Pagan temples. Much of Leviticus deals with the Holiness Code which outlined ways in which the ancient Hebrews were to be set apart to God. Some fertility worship practices found in nearly Pagan cultures were specifically prohibited; ritual same-sex behavior in Pagan temples was one such practice.

Read Leviticus 20:13. What is your reaction?
• The King James translation of Leviticus 20:13 is this:

If a man also lie with mankind, as he lieth with a woman, both of them have committed an abomination: they shall surely be put to death; their blood shall be upon them.

• Of course, Leviticus 20:13 is very similar to Leviticus 18:22; the major difference is the addition of a death penalty for those men who have gay sex. But, of course, questions about the correct translations and interpretations of these verses arise.
• One thing to note is that this verse says nothing about same-sex sexual relationships between two women.

• A good source to consult is this:

http://www.religioustolerance.org/hom_bibh3.htm

This source points out the difficulty of translating and interpreting this passage.

• Another good source to consult is this:

Helminiak, Daniel A. *What the Bible Really Says About Homosexuality*. San Francisco, CA: Alamo Square Press, c1994. Foreword by John S. Spong.

• On July 3, 2004, I downloaded this information from http://www.religioustolerance.org/hom_bibh3.htm:

Some comments on the death penalty aspect of this passage by pastors and academics taking a liberal position are:

J. Nelson: "It is grounded in the old Jewish understanding that women are less worthy than men. For a man to have sex with another man 'as with a woman' insults the other man, because women are to be treated as property." She added that this passage is not part of the 10 Commandments, but merely part of almost 600 additional rules put forth via Israel's religious leaders.

D. Bartlett: "Nobody I know, even the most conservative, is saying homosexuals should be executed. I think people who think they take the Bible literally don't take it so literally as to want to execute people."

Krister Stendahl: "If you look at the whole chapter, a lot of things come in for capital punishment that no Southern Baptist would argue that capital punishment is appropriate for. So their reading is a little selective."

Read Romans 1:26. What is your reaction?

• The King James translation of Romans 1:26 is this:

For this cause God gave them up unto vile affections: for even their women did change the natural use into that which is against nature:

• A good source to consult is this:

http://www.religioustolerance.org/hom_bibc.htm

This source points out the difficulty of translating and interpreting this passage.

• Another good source to consult is this:

Helminiak, Daniel A. *What the Bible Really Says About Homosexuality*. San Francisco, CA: Alamo Square Press, c1994. Foreword by John S. Spong.

• On July 3, 2004, I downloaded this information from http://www.religioustolerance.org/hom_bibc3.htm:

As stated in 2 Peter 3:15-17, we have to be very careful when interpreting the writings of Paul. "As also in all his [Paul's] epistles, speaking in them of these things; in which are some things hard to be understood, which they that are unlearned and unstable wrest, as they do also the other scriptures, unto their own destruction." (KJV)

As stated by Dr. R.S. Truluck, "Paul's writings have been taken out of context and twisted to punish and oppress every identifiable minority in the world: Jews, children, women, blacks, slaves, politicians, divorced people, convicts, pro choice people, lesbians, gays, bisexuals, transsexuals, religious reformers, the mentally ill, and the list could go on and on. Paul is often difficult and confusing to understand.

A lot of Paul's writing is very difficult to translate. Since most of his letters were written in response to news from other people, reading Paul can be like listening to one side of a telephone conversation. We know, or think we know, what Paul is saying, but we have to guess what the other side has said."

[...]

For the vast majority of adults, those who are heterosexual, it is indecent for them to engage in homosexual activities. For the small minority of humans who are homosexual, it would be indecent for them to engage in heterosexual activities. As C. Ann Shepherd writes: "When the scripture is understood correctly, it seems to imply that it would be unnatural for heterosexuals to live as homosexuals, and for homosexuals to live as heterosexuals."

Read the following satire and state your honest reaction to what you read.

• This satire has been emailed many times and has appeared on many places on the WWW. No one is sure who its author is.

Letter To Dr. Laura

Dear Dr. Laura,

Thank you for doing so much to educate people regarding God's Law. I have learned a great deal from your show, and I try to share that knowledge with as many people as I can. When someone tries to defend the homosexual lifestyle, for example, I simply remind him that Leviticus 18:22 clearly states it to be an abomination. End of debate.

I do need some advice from you, however, regarding some of the specific laws and how to best follow them.

a) When I burn a bull on the altar as a sacrifice, I know it creates a pleasing odour for the Lord (Lev. 1:9). The problem is my neighbours. They claim the odour is not pleasing to them. Should I smite them?

b) I would like to sell my daughter into slavery, as sanctioned in Exodus 21:7. In this day and age, what do you think would be a fair price for her?

c) I know that I am allowed no contact with a woman while she is in her period of menstrual uncleanliness (Lev. 15:19-24). The problem is, how do I tell? I have tried asking, but most women take offence.

d) Lev. 25:44 states that I may indeed possess slaves, both male and female, provided they are purchased from neighbouring nations. A friend of mine claims that this applies to Mexicans, but not Canadians. Can you clarify? Why can't I own a few Canadians?

e) I have a neighbour who insists on working on the Sabbath. Exodus 35:2 clearly states he should be put to death. Am I morally obliged to kill him myself?

f) A friend of mine feels that even though eating shellfish is an abomination (Lev. 11:10), it is a lesser abomination than homosexuality. I don't agree. Can you settle this?

g) Lev. 21:20 states that I may not approach the altar of God if I have a defect in my sight. I have to admit that I wear reading glasses. Does my vision have to be 20/20, or is there some wiggle room here?

h) Most of my male friends get their hair trimmed, including the hair around their temples, even though this is expressly forbidden by Lev. 19:27. How should they die?

i) I know from Lev. 11:6-8 that touching the skin of a dead pig makes me unclean, but may I still play football if I wear gloves?

j) My uncle has a farm. He violates Lev. 19:19 by planting two different crops in the same field, as does his wife by wearing garments made of two different kinds of thread (cotton/polyester blend). He also tends to curse and blaspheme a lot. Is it really necessary that we go to all the trouble of getting the whole town together to stone them? (Lev. 24:10-16) Couldn't we just burn them to death at a private family affair like we do with people who sleep with their in-laws? (Lev. 20:14)

I know you have studied these things extensively, so I am confident you can help. Thank you again for reminding us that God's word is eternal and unchanging.

Your devoted disciple and adoring fan.

Chapter 16

What is Chad's reaction to Annie and Liza's relationship?

• Chad takes it fairly well, I suppose.

• At first, he barely speaks to Liza, and when he does speak, he doesn't look at her.

• Mrs. Poindexter calls him into her office, and she questions him about Liza.

• Basically, Chad lies to protect Liza. He doesn't tell about Liza and Annie holding hands, and he replies, "I don't know," to questions about Liza and boys.

• Liza tells Chad the truth. Later, she hears Chad crying at night.

How fair is the "trial" of Liza?

• The trial is a trustees' meeting.

• Liza does not have a lawyer; Ms. Widmer and Ms. Stevenson do.

• All three of the accused wear dresses — Liza feels that it is as they are all saying, "Look! We're women!" She feels that is ridiculous.

• Ms. Baxter is a hypocrite. As a Christian, she talks about believing the best of everyone, but she seems to believe the worst of Annie, Liza, Ms. Widmer, and Ms. Stevenson.

• The red-haired woman trustee is a sympathetic character, since she is sympathetic to Liza. She remarks drily that Ms. Baxter made the original complaint after Ms. Baxter says that it is difficult to talk about such things (certainly the difficulty didn't keep Ms. Baxter from making the original complaint).

• The red-haired woman trustee also doesn't want Liza to reveal Annie's name — after all, Annie is not a Foster Academy student.

• Ms. Turner is opposed to Ms. Baxter, who acts as if she is pious, and the red-haired woman looks as if Ms. Baxter were "something she would like to squash under her heel" (203).

• Ms. Baxter is obviously putting her own slant on what she saw.

• Fortunately, the red-haired woman especially makes Ms. Baxter testify as to what she actually saw.

• Mr. Turner does want Liza to testify — to talk — instead of her parents. He does say that her parents can assist her, and that they can withdraw any time they think they need counsel.

• Liza tries to remember the words to "Invictus," and the words — but nothing else — seem to help her.

• Mr. Turner wants for Ms. Poindexter to be quiet while Liza is speaking; after all, Liza was quiet while Ms. Baxter was speaking.

• Liza's mom tries to defend her. Liza's mom still is trying to come up with an innocent explanation for what happened.

• When Mrs. Poindexter asks why Liza and Annie were wearing so little, Liza says that she needs a lawyer. Mrs. Poindexter says that that answer can be interpreted as an admission of guilt.

• Mr. Turner clears his throat angrily, and the red-haired woman blows up. She is enlightened about homosexuality. She doesn't care what Annie and Liza did off of school grounds and not during school time.

• The trial turns to the two teachers: Ms. Widmer and Ms. Stevenson.

• The red-haired woman does make one mistake. She says that whatever Liza and Annie did is of no importance. Of course, to Liza and Annie, what they did — love each other — is of great importance.

• Liza does make one mistake. She wants to tell the trustees that Ms. Widmer and Ms. Stevenson had no influence on her and Annie, but understandably she can't bring herself to do it. She is intimidated.

Chapter 17

How do other Foster Academy students treat Chad?

• Chad is in a fight once. He comes home with a bloody hair and with blood in his hair. Neither Chad nor Liza's dad — whom Chad runs to — ever tell Lisa what happened. However, Liza can guess what happened.

• Chad walks with Liza to school when she is allowed to return — no disciplinary actions are taken against her at all; she is still Student Council President. He walks with her into the school, although Liza says that he can go into school separately if he wants. He tells her that if she needs help to just ask — he has a good left jab. He also stares hard at a couple of students who look funny at Liza. Liza hugs Chad in the hall.

What are the reactions of the students to Annie and Liza's relationship?

• Things are strained at school. Both Liza and the other students feel awkward. Of course, we can guess that lots of students have been gossiping about Liza.

• A student named Valerie Crabb tries to be friendly, saying that if Liza needs help in getting caught up in physics to ask her.

• When Liza goes into the ladies room, someone says, "HI, LIZA" loudly — it is a warning to other students. Probably they have been gossiping about her. Or the speaker may be warning other students that a lesbian is present.

• Walt is kind of a jerk. He tries to be friendly, but he regards being lesbian as being deviant.

• Zelda, Liza's lab partner, asks her what two girls do in bed. She has an audience when she asks that. (Zelda is going to be a doctor.)

• Girls don't want to sit near Liza in class.

• Liza admits that there are only a few bad students. And for each bad student, there are at least two who are very nice. Many students treat her just the same as always.

What happens to Mrs. Poindexter?

• Mrs. Poindexter is fired because of overreactions to trivial events and frequent demonstrations of poor judgment. Also, "continuous overextension of authority to the point of undermining democratic principles" (219-220). Mrs. Poindexter will leave at the end of the year.

• Liza learns this information from a student named Conn.

How does Sally treat Liza?

• Sally thinks that Liza is a pervert. She says that Walt knows of a good doctor who can treat homosexuals.

• Sally feels justified in what she did.

• Sally thinks that it is a good thing that Ms. Widmer and Ms. Stevenson have been fired.

• Sally thinks that Ms. Widmer and Ms. Stevenson must have influenced Liza to become gay.

• Liza points out that she didn't even know that Ms. Widmer and Ms. Stevenson were gay. Therefore, Liza would have been gay even if she had never known Ms. Widmer and Ms. Stevenson.

• Sally thinks that "gay" is "a terribly sad word" (222).

• Liza points out that being "gay" is about love, that it is about relationships with other human beings.

• Sally testified at the hearing about Ms. Widmer and Mr. Stevenson. Sally thinks that Liza idolized those two teachers and was influenced by them, that Liza felt that anything they did was OK.

If you feel like doing research, investigate an example of gay-bashing (for example, the death of Matthew Shepherd) and explain what you find out.

On July 4, 2004, I downloaded this information from

http://liberalslikechrist.org/about/
homophobia.html:Matthew Shepherd was a kind, gentle
and unassuming young college student, until he crossed the
path of the wrong "normal" people. Matt was viciously
beaten and then tied much like "the good thief" to a fence,
and left there to suffer alone and die. What makes Matt's
case stand out from the hundreds of other such cases is his
funeral, because several dedicated so-called "Christians"
went out of their way to attend his funeral in Laramee,
Wyoming and to demonstrate with their signs and their
shouting their firm belief that "God hates fags." They
succeeded in communicating their message of hate, not only
to Terry's family and community, but to the whole world
through the television coverage they rightfully expected this
funeral would receive.

The Rev. [Fred] Phelps who inspired this (and many other
such demonstrations) has dedicated his life to this
"ministry," using among other tools, his internet site, where
he proudly display[s] a daily count of how many days
Matthew Shepherd ha[s] supposedly been in hell.

Interlude

What happens during this short interlude?

• Liza feels guilty about not doing more to stand up for Ms. Widmer and Ms. Stevenson. They had no effect on Liza's being gay. Liza would have been gay no matter what.

• An important thing that happens is that Liza admits that she is gay. She also knows that she loves Annie in a way that she could not if she weren't gay.

Chapter 18

How are Ms. Widmer and Ms. Stevenson affected by the discovery of their relationship?

• Ms. Widmer and Ms. Stevenson are both fired and have to find other jobs.

• Ms. Widmer and Ms. Stevenson do treat Liza and Annie well.

• Ms. Widmer and Ms. Stevenson move away. They have a place in the country where they were going to retire. They are moving there.

• Probably neither Ms. Widmer nor Ms. Stevenson will ever teach again.

What happened to Ms. Widmer and Ms. Stevenson earlier in their lives?

• When Ms. Widmer and Ms. Stevenson were young, their parents suspected that they were gay and in love, and so they were forbidden to see each other. Of course, they did anyway.

• Ms. Stevenson was a WAC. (WAC means "Women's Army Corp.") Someone found some of Ms. Widmer's letters to her. There was an investigation.

• Ms. Stevenson was discharged, and she found it difficult to find a college that would accept her. Eventually, one did, and after Ms. Stevenson had graduated and found a job, the discharge had no practical effect on her life.

• Ms. Widmer blamed herself for the discharge — she had written the letters. Their relationship almost broke up because of that.

How good is the advice that Ms. Widmer and Ms. Stevenson give to Annie and Liza in chapter 18?

• Liza is still thinking about Annie in the interlude in this chapter.

• Ms. Stevenson says:

There are a lot of unfair things in this world, and gay people certainly come in for their share of them — but so do lots of other people, and besides, it doesn't really matter. What matters is the truth of loving, of two people finding each other. That's what's important, and don't you forget it." (229)

• Liza feels good being with other gay people and being able to hold Annie's hand in their presence.
• Ms. Widmer and Ms. Stevenson say that they will make it through the bad times.
• Ms. Widmer and Ms. Stevenson tell Liza and Annie some good advice.

Ms. Stevenson says:

"Bad things can always be overcome." (232)

Ms. Widmer says:

"If you two remember nothing else from all this, remember that. Please. Don't — don't punish yourselves for people's ignorant reactions to what we all are." (232)

Ms. Stevenson says:

"Don't let ignorance win. Let love." (232)

Ending

Does *Annie on My Mind* have a happy ending?

- Yes. Finally, Liza calls Annie. Annie will be home for Christmas vacation. They tell each other that they love each other.

- Liza says that the truth will set you free, and the truth is that she loves Annie. It is also true that Annie loves Liza.

- This is a very happy ending.

Bibliography

Carter, Judy. *The Homo Handbook*. New York: Fireside Books, 1996.

"Cloister." Dictionary.com. <http://dictionary.reference.com/browse/cloister>. Accessed 21 July 2013.

Ford, Michael Thomas. *Outspoken: Role Models from the Lesbian and Gay Community*. New York: Morrow Junior Books, 1998.

Fricke, Aaron. *Reflections of a Rock Lobster: A Story About Growing Up Gay*. Boston, MA: AlyCat Books, 1981.

Garbo. *The Complete Garbo Talks*. Columbus, OH: Big Breakfast Publishing, 1991.

Garden, Nancy. *Annie on My Mind*. New York: Farrar, Straus and Giroux, 1982.

Garden, Nancy. *Lesbian and Gay Stories of Struggle, Progress, and Hope, 1950 to the Present*. New York: Farrar Straus Giroux, 2007.

Holman, C. Hugh, and William Harmon. *A Handbook to Literature*. 6th ed. New York: Macmillan Publishing Company, 1992.

Marcovitz, Hal. *Bruce Coville*. Philadelphia, PA: Chelsea House Publishers, 2006.

Orleans, Ellen. *Can't Keep a Straight Face*. Bala Cynwyd, PA: Laugh Lines Press, 1992.

Perry, Joel. *Funny That Way: Adventures in Fabulousness*. Los Angeles, CA: Alyson Books, 2001.

Signorile, Michelangelo. *Outing Yourself: How to Come Out as Lesbian or Gay to Your Family, Friends, and Coworkers*. New York: Simon and Schuster, 1995.

Vilanch, Bruce. *Bruce! Adventures in the Skin Trade and Other Essays*. New York: Jeremy P. Tarcher/Putnam, 2000.

Warren, Roz, editor. *Revolutionary Laughter: The World of Women Comics*. Freedom, CA: The Crossing Press, 1995.

Paper Topics

• Discuss how Liza and Annie's love develops during the course of the novel.

• Discuss the theme of homophobia as it appears in the novel.

• If you feel like doing research, find and read one or more coming-out stories (stories in which a homosexual reveals that he or she is gay). What is your reaction to the story or stories you have researched? You may research happy coming-out stories, sad coming-out stories, or a combination of both. Google "coming-out stories" or "comingout stories" or "coming out stories.) Here are two good sources to use:

https://whenicameout.com
http://www.bibble.org/gay/stories/comingout.html

Appendix A: Anecdotes

If a teacher is able to get a laugh or two in the classroom, great! And if the laughs are relevant to the subject matter, even better!

Here are a few Nancy Garden and gay and lesbian anecdotes that teachers are welcome to retell in the classroom as relevant. These anecdotes have appeared in my collections of anecdotes, which are gay- and lesbian-friendly books.

Nancy Garden

• Gay and lesbian activists sometimes have to fight scary battles. In the 1960s, some members of the American Nazi Party wanted to cause trouble at a conference of ECHO (East Coast Homophile Organizations). The gays and lesbians banded together to keep the American Nazis out of the auditorium where the conference was being held by locking arms and forming a human barricade that refused to let the American Nazis through. Among the activists barricading the door was Nancy Garden, lesbian author of *Annie on My Mind*.

Source: Nancy Garden, *Lesbian and Gay Stories of Struggle, Progress, and Hope, 1950 to the Present*, p. 50.

• The responses author Nancy Garden has received to her book *Annie on My Mind*, which portrays lesbian characters in a positive manner, have been mostly supportive. For example, she once received a letter from a straight teenage girl who had been asked by her mother, a newspaper reporter, to read the book in order to find out an average teenager's response to the book. At first, the girl didn't want to read about "those people," but she enjoyed the book and wrote Ms. Garden, "Those girls are just like any other girls falling in love." Ms. Garden says, "That was great, because that's exactly what I wanted to say in the book."

Source: Michael Thomas Ford, *Outspoken*, p. 63.

• Among the dumb beliefs many people have held about gays and lesbians (about as dumb as the belief in the secret handshake) is that gays and lesbians wear green on Thursdays, aka Fairy Day. In the 1960s, this belief amused Nancy Garden, the future author of the lesbian love story *Annie on My Mind* (it has a happy ending!). She wore green every day she attended school because her school uniform was green.

Source: Nancy Garden, *Lesbian and Gay Stories of Struggle, Progress, and Hope, 1950 to the Present*, p. 47.

Gays and Lesbians

• The mother of comedian Liz Feldman knew that Liz was a lesbian even before Liz figured it out. At age 16, Liz went away from home to a summer drama program at which a girl seduced her. Liz knew then that she liked girls, but at the time she thought she also liked boys. The following summer she went to another drama program, and her mother walked into Liz's room and saw two girls sleeping together in bed. Ironically, the girls weren't gay; they were just tired. One month later, Liz stayed the night at one of the girls' houses, and when she returned home her mother told her, "There's a letter on your bed ... it's from me." Her mother also told her, "Don't open it here — open it in the car!" In the car, which Liz was not allowed to drive, she opened the letter, in which were two poems. The first poem was written from the perspective of a daughter who comes out to her mother and says that she's gay. Not ready yet to talk, Liz simply told her mother, "You're very perceptive." The second poem was written from the perspective of a mother talking to her gay daughter, saying, "It's OK, we'll figure it out, I still love you." Both poems rhymed. Liz didn't want her mother to tell her father, who believed that being gay was a mental disease, but her mother told her father anyway. Her father took her to get a psychiatric evaluation, and the therapist asked, "What's the problem?" Liz replied, "That's just it. I don't think it's a problem. Everybody else thinks it's a problem, but I just wish we would stop using the word 'problem.'" Liz is justly proud today of how she handled this situation at age 17. After the psychiatric evaluation, Liz says, "The therapist said I was the most mentally stable teenager she'd ever had in her office and that I didn't need therapy, but that she recommended that my parents stay on" to get some help in adjusting to their daughter's gayness. Her father was proud of Liz's psychiatric evaluation. He told her, "Most mentally stable kid, look at you!" He also tossed her the keys to the family car, and that was the first time she was allowed to drive it. As a 30-year-old adult, Liz made this coming-out story into a short movie. To protect his privacy, her father does not appear in the film, which is titled "My First Time Driving." Liz says, "I made the film with my sister, which was also a dream come true. I always wanted to work with my sister; we're very close and get along really beautifully."

Source: Karman Kregloe, "Interview With Liz Feldman." 6 April 2008

http://www.afterellen.com/people/2008/4/lizfeldman

• Pratibha Parmar, the director of *Nina's Heavenly Delights* and other movies, finds her content in subjects such as lesbians, women, and South Asians. She has a happy relationship with her partner, and her movie *Nina's Heavenly Delights* tells a positive lesbian love story. She says, "In my own life I have a very happy, full relationship with my partner. I've had that for many years, and I know many other lesbians who do, so why do we always have to be portrayed as psychos or dysfunctional women? Why [are we not portrayed] just like anyone else? We fall in love and yeah, we go through our struggles, but also we have a potential to live happily ever after." By showing positive portrayals of lesbians, *Nina's Heavenly Delights* reflects reality. For example, in the summer of 2006, Ms. Parmar and her partner attended a civil partnership ceremony for two lesbians they know. She says, "The two women were both Indian, and they'd had their outfits made and embroidered in India. Both their families were there, their uncles and their aunts and their mums and dads and their nephews, kids running around. It was like a typical Indian wedding except that there were two brides. Now that is progress. That is change. So my film [*Nina's*

Heavenly Delights] isn't just complete fantasy; things like that do happen."

Source: Sharon Hadrian, "Pratibha Parmar Makes Change." 6 June 2007

http://www.afterellen.com/people/2007/6/pratibhaparmar

• George Takei's fellow actors on *Star Trek* accept his homosexuality. (Mr. Takei played Sulu on the original TV series of *Star Trek*.) When the *Star Trek* movies began to be made, Mr. Takei would bring his partner, Brad Altman, to the Friday-night wrap parties after a week's work was done. The first time he introduced Mr. Altman as a "friend," but he kept bringing Mr. Altman to the parties. Mr. Takei says about his fellow workers in TV and movies, "They're sophisticated people, so they put two and two together and said, 'Hmmm, I get it.'" He discovered that Walter Koenig, the actor who played Pavel Chekov, knew that he was gay when Mr. Koenig motioned for him to turn around one day. Mr. Takei did turn around, and he saw a "stunningly good-looking young extra wearing the tight *Star Trek* uniform." Immediately, Mr. Takei thought, "Okay, Walter knows and Walter understands." Mr. Koenig and his wife also invited Mr. Takei over to visit them, saying, "Why don't you bring Brad over?" Therefore, Mr. Takei says that his outing "happened in a very normal, natural, friendly way."

Source: Michael Jensen, "Interview with George Takei and Brad Altman. Afterelton.com. 18 June 2008

http://www.afterelton.com/people/2008/6/
georgetakei_bradaltman

• Marion Dane Bauer once invited fellow young adult writers to submit short stories for a book about gay teenagers. Bruce Coville wrote "Am I Blue?" — which became the title story of the book, whose full title is *Am I Blue? Coming Out from the Silence*. Mr. Coville is a happily married heterosexual, and his story is about a narrator who is beaten up by the school bully, Butch, because Butch thinks that the narrator is gay. An effeminate fairy godfather named Melvin visits the narrator and gives him the power of seeing whether someone is gay. A person who is totally gay will be dark blue, and a person who is wondering if he or she is gay will be light blue. The narrator's skin is light blue, and as he looks around he sees that a man whom everyone "knows" is straight is dark blue and he sees that a woman whom everyone "knows" is a lesbian is not blue at all. When the narrator looks at Butch, he sees that Butch is dark blue.

Source: Hal Marcovitz, *Bruce Coville*, pp. 94, 96.

• One of *Tucson Weekly* columnist Tom Danehy's friends was an almost flamboyantly gay man also named Tom, who worked a couple of days a week at Blockblocker in addition to holding down another job. Gay Tom was a movie buff. Mr. Danehy says that often customers would come in looking for something like *Saw XXVII* but gay Tom would convince them to rent a true suspense classic such as *Dial 'M' for Murder* instead. In fact, gay Tom would follow customers around in the video store, and he would often say about a customer's choice, "Don't take that!" Then gay Tom would guide the customers to the "classics" section and convince them to rent something that truly exemplified excellence.

Source: Tom Danehy, "My friend is gone, three decades too early." *Tucson Weekly*. 8 November 2007

http://www.tucsonweekly.com/gbase/Opinion/ Content?oid=oid:102916

• In 1999, Duke University was not known for tolerance of homosexuality; instead, homosexuality was virtually invisible on campus. This bothered Lucas Schaefer, Leila Nesson Wolfrum, and a few of their friends, and they decided to take action. Figuring that the problem was not outright discrimination against gays and lesbians, but rather a refusal to acknowledge their existence, they designed and ordered a T-shirt that bore the message "gay? fine by me." Soon, lots of people were wearing these T-shirts, thus acknowledging both that homosexuals exist and that lots of people were OK with that fact.

Source: Greg Bloom, "Fine by Us." 30 November 2006

http://www.campusprogress.org/features/1306/fine-by-us

• Movies are rated G, PG, R, and X; so are movie trailers. Gay comedy writer Bruce Vilanch noticed that the movie trailer for *Chasing Amy* was rated R because of a brief kiss between two women — the trailer had no violence, drug use, or bad language. However, movie trailers rated G showed such things as dinosaurs trying to eat people, men with guns shooting other men with guns, and people screaming as their cars head straight toward a cliff.

Source: Bruce Vilanch, *Bruce! Adventures in the Skin Trade and Other Essays*, p. 67.

• Gays and lesbians can be *Star Wars* fanatics, too. In England, a lesbian couple wanted their wedding cake to display the Death Star from the movie *Star Wars*. The bakery at first declined to create a cake like that, until one lesbian exclaimed, "Look, it's my big gay wedding and we want a Death Star!" By the way, model makers created the spaceships for George Lucas' *Star Wars* by using parts from model kits for such vehicles as Kenworth Tractors, Panzer Kampfwagens, a Ford Galaxy 500 XL, and Kandy-Vans.

Source: Paul Constant, "In a 'Star Trek' Outfit (How Not to Get Married." *The Stranger*. 24 June 2008

http://www.thestranger.com/seattle/Content?oid=606110

Also: Sally Kline, editor, *George Lucas: Interviews*, p. 51.)

• Gay author Joel Perry recommends being out of the closet so gays and lesbians can fight for their rights. Of course, he realizes that being out means possibly being targeted for abuse, but even that can be an opportunity for activism. For example, if a bigot calls him a queer, he corrects the bigot by saying that he is a "fantastic queer."

Source: Joel Perry, *Funny That Way: Adventures in Fabulousness*, p. 86.

• Bill Serpe of Milwaukee, Wisconsin, came out when he was 24 years old, although he had realized that he was gay at age 19. For five years, he led a double life, talking at his day job as a shoe salesman about dating women although at night he was really dating men. One day, his boss asked him what he had done the evening before, and Mr. Serpe replied that he had been on a date. That's when he realized that he couldn't keep lying, that he had to be open about his sexuality. When his boss asked what her name was, Mr. Serpe replied, "His name was John." His father was in denial about Mr. Serpe's sexuality, and although they discussed it once, they didn't discuss it further for a very long time. When Mr. Serpe was 29 years old, at Thanksgiving he visited his family, then he left to see his partner. His father asked, "Why don't you pick her up and bring her back here?" Mr. Serpe replied, "It's not a her." Hearing this, his stepmother asked, "Then why don't you bring him back here?" That's when Mr. Serpe came out to the rest of his family. He says, "It was difficult at first, but we worked through it. I've been a very lucky gay man."

Source: Lisa Kaiser, "'It's the Most Liberating Thing': Six Milwaukeeans tell their coming-out stories." *The Shepherd Express*. 7 June 2007

http://shepherd-express.com/
1editorialbody.lasso?-token.folder=2007-06-07&-token.story=177343.11312

• As a gay teenager, Paul Guilbert showed little fear. Whenever someone called him "faggot," he would reply, "That's right, honey." (And whenever someone hit him, he hit back.) Mr. Guilbert was Aaron Frick's date at his high school prom, which Mr. Fricke writes about in *Reflections of a Rock Lobster: A Story About Growing Up Gay.*

Source: Aaron Fricke, *Reflections of a Rock Lobster: A Story About Growing Up Gay*, p. 44.

• Film critic and entertainment journalist Lydia Marcus knew a boy named Robert who was gay and who came out in an interesting way. He didn't use words, but when he was 14 years old, he visited Lydia's house while wearing his mother's big white hat and her pedal-pusher pants. This was enough for both Lydia and her parents to know that he was gay. In the ninth grade, he came out to his classmates. Again, he didn't use words, but he did go to school wearing a white sweatshirt *Flashdance*-style, with the low-cut scoop neckline revealing a naked shoulder. This was enough to draw large amounts of attention to him at lunchtime. Lots of people who are aware of homophobia might advise Robert to learn how to run fast, but fortunately he knew how to fight anyone who attempted to harass him, so he didn't have to learn how to run.

Source: Lydia Marcus, "Of course Betty's nephew is gay." 18 December 2006

http://www.advocate.com/exclusive_detail_ektid40350.asp

• Like heterosexual couples, gay couples have stories about how they got engaged. In 2004, on New Year's Eve, Amber and Carol were playing Trivial Pursuit with two friends. When the clock struck midnight, Carol knelt and tried to propose — she tried because in the middle of the proposal, Amber yelled, "You're doing it now? It's happening now?" Yes, it was happening, and yes, Amber said yes. Amber and Carol began to share the last name of Dennis after getting married on July 4, 2006.

Source: Jes Burns, "Tales of Commitment: Same-sex couples tell their stories." 11 January 2007

http://www.eugeneweekly.com/2007/01/11/weddings4.html

• Because of bans on gay marriages, even gays and lesbians in committed relationships run into problems. For example, Dana and Kelsey were in a committed lesbian relationship for 17 years — a relationship that ended only with Kelsey's death from cancer. Kelsey's parents had disowned her for many years, but in her final weeks of life they arrived on the scene and ordered the hospital to ban Dana from seeing Kelsey, despite Kelsey's wish to see her. Fortunately, because of a kind night shift, Dana was able to sneak into Kelsey's hospital room at night and visit her. When Kelsey died, her parents went to the home of Dana and Kelsey and took away Kelsey's possessions — and Dana's. However, Dana was able to get revenge on Kelsey's parents for the way they had treated her. When the hospital telephoned Dana about paying tens of thousands of dollars of medical debt not covered by Kelsey's insurance, Dana replied, "I'm not family. You need to call Kelsey's parents."

Source: Michael Abernethy, "Queer, Isn't It?: PFLAG: A Piece of Our Hearts." 16 October 2007

http://www.popmatters.com/pm/columns/article/49482/pflag-a-piece-of-our-hearts/

• In 1983, during Thanksgiving weekend, Catholic parents Casey and Mary Ellen Lopata discovered that their oldest son, Jim, a sophomore in college, was lonely. He told his mother, "Mom, I'm lonely. I'm lonely for another man." This was how Mary Ellen realized that her son was gay, and she told him that his being gay didn't matter and that she loved him. He asked, "Then why are you crying?" She replied, "I don't know." His father didn't know what to say to him. He asked, "Are you sure?" and "Can you change?" Then he remained silent, wondering if his oldest son could be gay and still be a Catholic. As it turned out, Casey and Mary Ellen Lopata took a long time — nine years — to be comfortable while being open about having a gay son, but eventually they did become comfortable. In addition, they rejected neither their son nor their religion. In fact, Mary Ellen wrote a book titled *Fortunate Families: Catholic Families with Lesbian Daughters and Gay Sons* about Catholics learning to be open about having gay children. Together, she and her husband founded a group called Fortunate Families to help Catholic parents with gay children. Casey and Mary Ellen Lopata believe that their family has been fortunate in having a gay son, and they believe that having a gay son has made them better Catholics.

Source: Deb Price, "Catholic Parents of Gay Kids Find a Comfort Zone." Creators Syndicate. 28 October 2007

http://www.creators.com/opinion/deb-price/catholic-parents-of-gay-kids-find-a-comfort-zone.html

• The TV series *Queer Eye for the Straight Guy*, which aired on Bravo, opened up a lot of eyes — and minds. Many straight viewers of the series became aware that gay people can be very likeable; after all, the five stars of the series were and are very likeable. Kyan Douglas, the grooming expert, has received many, many letters about how grandmothers and grandfathers and Republicans watch the show, and so, he says, "I knew that we had some sort of impact on a part of society that just normally wouldn't have been exposed to gay people at all." Jai Rodriguez, the culture expert, has heard from a young gay man whose family was very religious and at first didn't care for gay people. However, they started watching and enjoying the *Queer Eye* series, and that made it easier for the young man to tell his family that he was gay. Of course, the show has had benefits for its stars. In addition to becoming famous celebrities, they have been able to come out of the closet in a global way, including to all their family relatives. Ted Allen, the food expert, says that the series "was a real gift for my mother because none of my relatives will ever again ask her why I'm not married or don't have a girlfriend."

Source: James Hillis, "A Look Back at Bravo's 'Queer Eye.'" 9 October 2007

http://www.afterelton.com/TV/2007/10/queereye

• Tim Gill is a gay business executive of the company that manufactures Quark XPress. He found coming out very difficult. While attending college in Boulder, Colorado, he walked into the Boulder Gay Liberation office, said "Hi," then "Hello," then he "just shook for ten minutes." Fortunately, the man in the office managed to calm him down. Like many other gay men of the time, Mr. Gill saw a psychiatrist. At this time, 1972, homosexuality was no longer considered aberrant, so the psychiatrist told him, "Well, if you want to change, I will help you. Otherwise, we just have to work on your parents."

Source: Michael Thomas Ford, *Outspoken*, pp. 193ff.

• Terry and Bill are a gay couple who have been together for over 25 years. Because they got together in the days before gays and lesbians could be legally married, they made up a date for their anniversary, choosing the first Friday in January because that is when they had their first date. Of course, the date of their anniversary changes from year to year, but they are original, after all. Each time the first Friday of January rolls around, they celebrate by eating at a nice restaurant. More and more, people are accepting homosexuality. Terry and Bill live in Lakewood, Washington, and they celebrated an anniversary in a nice restaurant in Steilacoom. Their male waiter overheard them toast each other, so he brought them a complimentary dessert and wished them, "Happy anniversary." For both Terry and Bill, it was a special night.

Source: "A Gay Valentine's Day. 13 February 2008

http://www.afterelton.com/people/2008/2/valetinesday

• Carol and Marie, a lesbian couple, once looked at a one-bedroom apartment in the company of Mrs. Hosserschall, a 70-year-old landlady. They were worried about what Mrs. Hosserschall's reaction to them might be, but she was extremely nice. They decided to take the apartment, and Marie asked the very butch Carol to get the checkbook and pay the down payment. Mrs. Hosserschall said, "That's right. Let your husband do it." Marie replied, "Carol's not, uh, we're not — she's not my husband, she's my girlfriend." Mrs. Hosserschall then asked if Carol paid her bills. Marie said that she did, so Mrs. Hosserschall said, "Well, then, she'd better get the checkbook before somebody rents the apartment out from under you."

Source: Garbo, *The Complete Garbo Talks*, pp. 83-84.

• Coming out can cause emotional distress in families, but many families eventually — and sometimes quickly — find a way of dealing with it. One family at first took hard the news of learning that their son was gay, but a couple of months later they told him, "We just want you to know that the reason we are struggling with this is that we are afraid of losing you. We don't want this issue to cause us to drift apart. And if there is anyone who has a problem with your being gay, they are no longer our friends. And that includes members of our extended family."

Source: Michelangelo Signorile, *Outing Yourself*, pp. 100-101.

• Gene is a gay man who is married and has two children; his wife, from whom he is separated, and his children all support him. His wife is his best friend, and when his son met at his high school a new girl who was curious about homosexuals and wanted to meet some "gay guys," his son knew exactly what to do. He invited her to his house so she could meet his father, Gene.

Source: Michael Abernethy, "Queer, Isn't It?: PFLAG: A Piece of Our Hearts." 16 October 2007

http://www.popmatters.com/pm/columns/article/49482/pflag-a-piece-of-our-hearts/

• When *Out* magazine editor Sarah Pettit entered college, she walked up to a man who looked very gay to her and asked, "Excuse me, you're gay, aren't you?" After he replied that he was, she said, "Well, then take me to where the gay people are." They went to a party, and she met the first woman she ever dated.

Source: Michael Thomas Ford, *Outspoken*, p. 98.

• While in college, humor writer Ellen Orleans went to see a therapist because she didn't feel romantic with men. The therapist suggested that she make a date with a man, so she did — but the man she asked out was gay. (The gay man's lover wasn't threatened by the date — he knew that Ms. Orleans was a lesbian even before she did.)

Source: Ellen Orleans, *Can't Keep a Straight Face*, p. 77.

• Lesbian stand-up comedian Judy Carter wore her freedom-ring necklace to a store, where one of two men behind a counter said, "I like your necklace." This was a safe way for him to come out to her, while still remaining closeted to his boss.

Source: Judy Carter, *The Homo Handbook*, p. 63.

• Lesbian comedian Lea Delaria's mother and sister have learned to accept her homosexuality. When they attended one of her concerts, she told them, "Listen, if you feel out of place, just hold hands. You'll fit right in." They laughed.

Source: Roz Warren, editor, *Revolutionary Laughter*, p. 79.

• Movie star Bette Midler uses topical and local humor in her nightclub act. As she tours, she calls up gay hot lines and gay switchboards to get the names of local homophobes so she can make fun of them in her act in that city.

Source: Bruce Vilanch, *Bruce! Adventures in the Skin Trade and Other Essays*, pp. 33-34.

Appendix B: Short Reaction Memos

The questions in this short guide can be used in discussions; however, they can also be used for short reaction memos. For example, I do this at Ohio University. See below for the assignment and sample short reaction memos.

How Do I Complete the Reaction Memo Assignments?

During the quarter, you will have to write a series of short memos in which you write about the readings you have been assigned.

Each memo should be at least 250 words, not counting long quotations from the work of literature. Include a word count for each memo, although that is not normally part of the memo format.

Following the memo heading (To, From, Re, Date, Words), write the question you are answering and the part of the book that the question applies to.

You may answer one question or more than one question. I will supply you with a list of questions that you may answer

Note that a Works Cited list is needed if you use quotations.

For examples from my Great Books courses at Ohio University in Athens, Ohio, see below.

To: David Bruce

From: Jane Student
Re: *Odyssey*, Book 12 Reaction Memo
Date: Put Today's Date Here
Words: 323
***Odyssey*, Book 12: Is Odysseus a bad leader?**

This is an important question in the *Odyssey*. After all, Odysseus leads 12 ships and many men to Troy, but the ships are all destroyed and all of his men die and he returns home to Ithaca alone. Who is responsible for the deaths of Odysseus' men? Is Odysseus responsible for their deaths, or do the men bear some responsibility for their own deaths? Many readers prefer Odysseus, the great individualist, to Aeneas, the man who (with his second wife, Lavinia) founds the Roman people, but then they realize that all of Odysseus' men died, while Aeneas succeeded in bringing many Trojans to Italy. When readers think of that, they begin to have a greater respect for Aeneas.

From the beginning of the *Odyssey*, this has been an issue. The bard says that the men perished because of the "recklessness of their own ways" (1.8). However, we notice that Odysseus is asleep at odd times. In Book 10, Aeolus gives Odysseus a bag in which the contrary winds have been tied up. This allows Odysseus to sail to Ithaca safely. However, they reach the island and see smoke rising from the fires, Odysseus goes to sleep and his men open the bag, letting the contrary winds escape, and the ship is blown back to King Aeolus' island. Similarly, in Book 12, on the island of the Sun-god, Odysseus is asleep when his men sacrifice the Sun-god's cattle.

It does seem that Odysseus does not bear the blame for his men's death. In many cases, they do perish through their own stupidity. In other cases, of course, they die during war or during adventures, but in those times, Odysseus was with them, and he could have died, too.

One other thing to think about is that Odysseus is telling his own story. Could he be lying? After all, some of the adventures he relates are pretty incredible. (Probably not. The gods vouch for some of what he says.)

Works Cited

Homer. *The Odyssey*. Trans. Robert Fagles. New York: Penguin Books, 1996. Print.

To: David Bruce

From: Jane Student

Re: *Inferno*, Canto 1 Reaction Memo

Date: Put Today's Date Here

Words: 263

***Inferno*, Canto 1**

• What do you need to be a member of the Afterlife in Dante's *Inferno*?

To be a member of the afterlife in Hell, you must meet a number of criteria:

1) You must be dead.
2) You must be an unrepentant sinner.
3) You must be a dead, unrepentant sinner by the year 1300.

Of course, only dead people — with a few exceptions such as Dante the Pilgrim — can be found in the Inferno.

Only unrepentant sinners can be found in the Inferno. Everyone has sinned, but sinners who repented their sins are found in Purgatory or Paradise, not in the Inferno.

Dante set his *Divine Comedy* in the year 1300, so the characters who appear in it are dead in the year 1300.

***Inferno*, Canto 1**

• What does it mean to repent?

A sinner who repents regrets having committed the sin. The repentant sinner vows not to commit the sin again, and he or she does his or her best not to commit the sin again.

***Inferno*, Canto 1**

• What is the geography of Hell? In *The Divine Comedy*, where is Hell located?

Hell is located straight down. We will find out later that when Lucifer was thrown out of Paradise, he fell to the Earth, ending up at the center of the Earth. The center of the Earth is the lowest part of Hell. Lucifer created the Mountain of Purgatory when he hit the Earth.

To: David Bruce

From: Jane Student

Re: *Candide*, Ch. 26-30

Date: Today's Date

Words: 368

Ch. 30: Write a brief character analysis of the old man and his family.

When Candide and his friends meet the old man, the old man is "sitting in front of his door beneath an arbor of orange trees, enjoying the fresh air" (119). The old man basically ignores politics that he cannot influence. Some people have recently been killed in Constantinople, and the old man does not even know their names. However, the old man does enjoy some material things, including good food, and he enjoys hospitality.

The old man invites Candide and his friends to enjoy some refreshments inside his house. They are served with "several kinds of fruit-favored drinks" and "boiled cream with pieces of candied citron in it, oranges, lemons, limes, pineapples, pistachio nuts, and mocha coffee" (119). The old man and his family have an abundance of food, but although Candide wonders if the old man has an enormous farm, the old man tells him, "I have only twenty acres of land, which my children and I cultivate. Our work keeps us free of three great evils: boredom, vice, and poverty" (119).

From this brief encounter, we learn several things:

- The old man and his family are content — even happy.

- The old man and his family ignore the wars and murders and crimes that happen elsewhere.

- The old man and his family have enough. They work hard on their little farm, and they have plenty of food and good things to eat.

• The old man and his family have only 20 acres, but 20 acres
are enough.

Candide and his friends decide to emulate the old man and his
family. Each of them begins to work hard on their little farm.
Cunegonde learns to make pastry, Paquette begins to embroider, and
the old woman does the laundry and repairs the linen. Brother Giroflée
becomes a carpenter, and Candide and the others grow "abundant
crops" (120). At the end of the short novel, the group of friends seem to
have come the closest they can to happiness in a world filled with evil,
but it does take an effort on their part. As Candide says in the short
novel's last words, "... we must cultivate our garden" (120).

Works Cited

Voltaire. *Candide*. Trans. Lowell Bair. New York: Bantam Books,
1981. Print.

To: David Bruce

From: Jane Student

Re: *A Connecticut Yankee in King Arthur's Court*, **Ch. 1-4 Reaction Memo**

Date: Put Today's Date Here

Words: 286

CH. 3: "KNIGHTS OF THE TABLE ROUND"

• What hints do we have of the relationship between Queen Guenever and Sir Launcelot?

Some hanky-panky is going on between Sir Launcelot and King Arthur's wife, Queen Guenever. Some six or eight prisoners address her, and they tell her that they have been captured by Sir Kay the Seneschal. Immediately, surprise and astonishment are felt by everybody present. The queen looks disappointed because she had hoped that the prisoners were captured by Sir Launcelot.

As it turns out, they were. Sir Launcelot first rescued Sir Kay from some attackers, then he took Sir Kay's armor and horse and captured more knights. All of these prisoners were actually captured by Sir Launcelot, not by Sir Kay at all.

Two passages let us know that something is going on between Sir Launcelot and Queen Guenever:

1. The first is subtle; she looks disappointed when Sir Kay says that he captured the knights: "Surprise and astonishment flashed from face to face all over the house; the queen's gratified smile faded out at the name of Sir Kay, and she looked disappointed ..." (503).

2. The other is much more overt and occurs after Guenever learns that the knight who really captured the prisoners was Sir Launcelot: "Well, it was touching to see the queen blush and smile, and look embarrassed and happy, and fling furtive glances at Sir Launcelot that would have got him shot in Arkansas, to a dead certainty" (503).

Works Cited

Twain, Mark. *Four Complete Novels*. New York: Gramercy Books, 1982. Print.

Appendix C: Debunking the Claims of the Anti-gay Marriage Crowd

For some years there has been a top ten list circulating in e-mail of items that handily debunk the silly claims of the anti-gay marriage crowd. I reproduce it for you here. [...]

1. Being gay is not natural. Real Americans always reject unnatural things like eyeglasses, polyester, and air conditioning.

2. Gay marriage will encourage people to be gay, in the same way that hanging around tall people will make you tall.

3. Legalizing gay marriage will open the door to all kinds of crazy behavior. People may even wish to marry their pets because a dog has legal standing and can sign a marriage contract.

4. Straight marriage has been around a long time and hasn't changed at all; women are still property, blacks still can't marry whites, and divorce is still illegal.

5. Straight marriage will be less meaningful if gay marriage were allowed; the sanctity of Britney Spears' 55-hour just-for-fun marriage would be destroyed.

6. Straight marriages are valid because they produce children. Gay couples, infertile couples, and old people shouldn't be allowed to marry because our orphanages aren't full yet, and the world needs more children.

7. Obviously, gay parents will raise gay children, since straight parents only raise straight children.

8. Gay marriage is not supported by religion. In a theocracy like ours, the values of one religion are imposed on the entire country. That's why we have only one religion in America.

9. Children can never succeed without a male and a female role model at home. That's why we as a society expressly forbid single parents to raise children.

10. Gay marriage will change the foundation of society; we could never adapt to new social norms. Just like we haven't adapted to cars, the service-sector economy, or longer life spans.

Source:
http://bluecollarscientist.com/2008/05/15/anti-gay-school-earns-a-hard-slapdown/
15 May 2008

Appendix D: Same-Sex Civil Marriage: Pro

By David Bruce

I am for same-sex civil marriage. Although I am not gay, some people erroneously think that I am gay. In part because of that reason, I tend to support gay rights, including the right of civil marriage. Because some people think that I am gay, I tend to have solidarity with gay people. In addition, I know some gays and lesbians, and I like them and realize that they are capable of long-term, committed, same-sex relationships. I would not deny them the ability to marry someone they love simply because they love someone of the same sex as themselves. In this paper, I will make some arguments for same-sex marriage, and I will rebut some arguments against same-sex marriage. Because many people's opposition to same-sex marriage rests on the incorrect assumption that homosexuality is against nature, I will also show that homosexuality is common among animals. When you finish reading this paper, I hope that you will agree with me that gays have the right to a civil marriage.

Arguments For Same-Sex Marriage

My main reason for wanting to allow same-sex couples to be legally joined in a civil marriage is that marriage is a way for committed couples, whether same sex or opposite sex, to show love and commitment to each other. Many same-sex couples have been together for years, are deeply in love, and wish to be married. Kathy Belge tells the story of how she came to be married to Tay, her partner of almost twelve years, in her article "A Lesbian Marriage: I Wed My True Love." In February 2004 she and her partner went to San Francisco in order to be legally married. At first, it seemed as if they would not be able to get married simply because of the number of same-sex couples waiting to be married. Ms. Belge writes that normally the mayor's office processed about 30 marriages in a normal day; however, after same-sex marriage became legal in San Francisco, the mayor's office had been processing about 400 marriages per day. Although it seemed that Ms. Belge and her partner would not be able to get married that day, they declined to leave. Their persistence paid off, and they were married later that day. Ms. Belge was so nervous that she held out the wrong hand for her partner to put the ring on. Ms. Belge had to take the ring off and put it on the correct hand. Ms. Belge writes,

> They say every woman dreams of her wedding day. As a child, I never did. But if I had, I don't think I could have imagined a day with more meaning. It meant so much to be able to share that moment with so many other couples. My wedding day, [sic] was not just about me and my beloved. It was about making a statement for the rights of people everywhere to be able to love whom they please. ("A Lesbian Marriage")

All adult same-sex couples who wish to be married should have the same right to be married in civil ceremonies as adult opposite-sex couples.

In addition, same-sex couples need to be married to enjoy important rights that heterosexual married couples have. Mary Bonauto, Project Director, Gay and Lesbian Advocates and Defenders (GLAD), wrote this on the GLAD Web site on 15 August 2003:

> While gay and lesbian families can protect themselves in limited ways by creating wills, health-care proxies and co-parent adoptions, this does not come close to emulating the automatic protections and peace of mind that marriage confers. People cannot contract their way into changing pension laws, survivorship rights, worker's-compensation

dependency protection or the tax system, to name just a few. (qtd. in Jost)

Evidence for this can be found in the experience of many gay and lesbian couples. For example, Bill Flanigan and Robert Daniel, who were a gay couple in San Francisco, protected themselves as much as possible by registering themselves as domestic partners under a San Francisco law. In addition, Mr. Daniel executed a health-care proxy. This proxy allowed Mr. Flanigan to make medical decisions for Mr. Daniel, who had AIDS. Unfortunately, on Oct. 16, 2000, Mr. Daniel was admitted to the University of Maryland's Shock Trauma Center in Baltimore, Maryland. Because Mr. Daniel and Mr. Flanigan were not legally married, and despite the health-care proxy that Mr. Daniel had executed, Mr. Flanigan was not allowed to see Mr. Daniel in his hospital room. Not until four hours had passed and Mr. Daniel's mother and sister arrived was Mr. Flanigan allowed to see Mr. Daniel. By then, Mr. Daniel was unconscious, and he died before the two men were able to say goodbye (Jost).

Legal marriage also gives other rights that gay and lesbian couples do not enjoy. For example, under the law marital communications are confidential: A spouse cannot be made to testify against his or spouse. Marriage also has important financial and tax benefits. For example, Richard Linnell has a health policy that covers the child whom he and his partner, Gary Chalmers, adopted, but to have Mr. Chalmers covered by the policy, Mr. Linnell has to pay extra (Jost). In addition, Gloria Bailey and Linda Davies, a lesbian couple, will have to pay taxes when they retire and sell their home and joint psychotherapy practice — taxes that a married couple would not have to pay (Jost).

Rebuttals of Arguments Against Same-Sex Marriage

One argument that is often made against legalizing same-sex marriage is that legalizing same-sex marriage would require churches to marry same-sex couples. This is not true. In the United States, the

First Amendment guarantees religious freedom: "Congress shall make no law respecting an establishment of religion, or prohibiting the free exercise thereof" (U.S. Constitution.) In the United States, church and state are separated. If Congress were to pass a law that legalized same-sex marriage, that law would apply only to civil marriages. Churches would still be able to marry whomever they wish, and they would still be able not to marry whomever they wish.

Another argument that is often made against same-sex marriage is that homosexuality is against God's wishes as revealed in the Bible. Those critics sometimes say that the book of Genesis tells us about Adam and Eve, not Adam and Steve. However, a Catholic priest who has argued well against this belief is Daniel A. Helminiak, author of *What the Bible* Really *Says About Homosexuality*. In his "Preface to the Millennium Edition," Helminiak says that the goal of his book, which was first printed in 1994, "was to make available in easily readable form a summary of a growing body of scholarly literature on homosexuality in the Bible. Even in 1994, the inevitable conclusion of the scholarly research was already clear. Taken on its own terms and in its own time, the Bible nowhere condemns homosexuality as we know it today" (13). Helminiak does not advocate a literal interpretation of the Bible in which "a text means whatever it means to somebody reading it today" (33). Instead, he advocates a historical-critical reading of the Bible in which "a text means whatever it meant to the people who wrote it long ago" (33). Both ways of reading the Bible agree that the Bible is the Word of God.

Should a text mean whatever it means to people today, or should it mean whatever it meant to the person or people who wrote it? Let's take a look at a passage from *The Silver Chair*, one of the children's novels in C.S. Lewis's Chronicles of Narnia, a series of books with Christian themes. The characters Puddleglum, Scrubb, and Jill are among some dangerous giants. Puddleglum wants the children Scrubb and Jill, as well as himself, to pretend to be "[a]s if we hadn't a care in the world. Frolicsome" (103). The children agree to the plan, and a little later we read this about Jill: "She made love to everyone — the grooms, the porters, the housemaids, the ladies-in-waiting, and the elderly giant lords whose hunting days were past. She submitted to being kissed and pawed about [...]" (107). How should we interpret the phrase "made love to" in this passage? To today's readers, "made love to" means "had sex with," but that hardly seems to be the best way to interpret this passage from a Christian novel for children. What did C.S. Lewis, the author of the passage, intend by the phrase? *The Silver Chair* was first published in 1953, when to make love to meant to flirt with someone and be charming. That meaning is obsolete now, but it is the meaning with which Lewis used the phrase. Jill is not having sex with all these characters in the novel; she is simply being charming and making them like her.

Possibly, someone could argue that God will make sure that the words in the Bible have the meaning that He wants them to have. However, this is incorrect. For example, a 1631 edition of the King James Bible contained this remarkable typo: "Thou shalt commit adultery" (its translation of Exodus 20:14); however, the translators had no ill intention (North). Because of this typo, this edition of the Bible is known as the "Wicked Bible."

When it comes to understanding what the Bible says about same-sex relationships, we have to understand what the authors of the Bible meant by same-sex relationships. In our modern culture, we know that gay men and gay women can have loving same-sex relationships. However, what is referred to in the Bible as homosexual acts are not of that kind. For example, in the story of Sodom (Genesis 19:1-19), the men of Sodom wanted to rape the angels to whom Lot was providing hospitality. Here the offense is rape and inhospitality, not a condemnation of homosexuality as we know it today. Helminiak writes, "Not homosexuality but hardheartedness is the offense of Gibeah [see Judges 19] and of Sodom" (47).

According to Leviticus 18:22, "You shall not lie with a male as with a woman; it is an abomination" (qtd. in Helminiak 51). Leviticus 20:13 states, "If a man lie with a man as with a woman, both of them have committed an abomination; they shall be put to death, their blood is upon them" (qtd. in Helminiak 51). Here the Bible condemns the penetration of one man sexually by another man, but Helminiak looks at the reasons why this kind of sex is condemned. The condemnation occurs in what is called the Holiness Code of Leviticus, which is concerned with keeping Israel "holy" in the sight of God (Helminiak 53). To be holy is to be set apart. The author of Leviticus was concerned with keeping the Jews different from the Gentiles. At the time, Gentiles such as the Canaanites permitted the penetration of one man sexually by another man. Helminiak writes, "The point is that The Holiness Code of Leviticus prohibits male same-sex acts for religion reasons, not for sexual reasons. The concern is to keep Israel distinct from the Gentiles. Homosexual sex is forbidden because it is associated with Gentile identity" (54). In the Common Era, of course, Christianity is a major religion of the Gentiles. Helminiak uses an analogy here. At one time Catholics did not eat meat on Friday. Of course, nothing is wrong with eating meat. But the Catholics were concerned with acting like Catholics and with not acting the same way as Protestants. A Catholic who then ate meat on Friday was guilty of an offense against a religious responsibility (55). Of course, a Catholic who now eats meat on Friday is not guilty of an offense against a religious responsibility.

Leviticus 20:13 advocates the death penalty for gay penetrative sex, and Leviticus 20:9 advocates the death penalty for cursing one's parents: "For every one that curseth his father or his mother shall be surely put to death: he hath cursed his father or his mother; his blood shall be upon him" (King James Version). Today, we do not advocate putting to death a person who curses his parents, nor do we advocate putting to death a person who is homosexual. The circumstances that led the writer of Leviticus to prescribe the death penalty for these actions have changed. By the way, the late Monty Python member Graham Chapman once appeared on a TV talk show, in which he discussed his homosexuality. A viewer wrote in to the talk show, enclosing in her letter some prayers for Chapman's soul, as well as the biblical injunction that if a man lie with another he shall be taken out and killed. Python member Eric Idle read the viewer's letter, then wrote her in reply, "We've taken him out and killed him!" (Hay 158).

Helminiak examines other Biblical passages that seem to condemn homosexuality; his book is well worth a read. Reading his book can make people much more accepting of gays and lesbians. For example, when gay author Michael Thomas Ford came out to his sister, her response was, "Well, you know I'm okay with it, but God says it's wrong, so you're probably going to hell" (Ford 115). If Ford's sister had read this book, she may not have said to her brother that he would probably go to hell.

An argument that is often made against homosexuality in general is that it is unnatural. However, homosexuality is widely practiced in nature by animals, as scientists are beginning to discover. Joan Roughgarden, a professor of biology at Stanford University, is one of several scientists who have studied homosexual behavior among non-human vertebrates. In the introduction to her book *Evolution's Rainbow: Diversity, Gender, and Sexuality in Nature and People*, Ms. Roughgarden writes, "Much of this book presents the gee-whiz of vertebrate diversity [including] how species incorporate same-sex courtship, including sexual contact, as regular parts of their social systems" (2). In an article about Ms. Roughgarden and her book, Jonah Lehrer wrote,

> Giraffes have all-male orgies. So do bottlenose dolphins, killer whales, gray whales, and West Indian manatees. Japanese macaques, on the other hand, are ardent lesbians; the females enthusiastically mount each other. Bonobos, one

of our closest primate relatives, are similar, except that their lesbian sexual encounters occur every two hours. Male bonobos engage in "penis fencing," which leads, surprisingly enough, to ejaculation. They also give each other genital massages. ("The Effeminate Sheep")

Ms. Roughgarden believes that sex has more than just the purpose of human reproduction; it can simply be a way to have fun or to create social bonds.

Other scientists have also studied the gay animal kingdom. Bruce Bagemihl spent ten years researching his book titled *Biological Exuberance: Animal Homosexuality and Natural Diversity*. Part of his book is devoted to showing the reaction of researchers when they realized that the animals that they were studying were gay. Susan McCarthy, in reviewing Bagemihl's book, wrote this: "One unusually candid biologist wrestled with the realization that the bighorn rams he studied frequently had sex with each other, and weren't just showing nice wholesome aggression. 'To state that the males had evolved a homosexual society was emotionally beyond me. To conceive of those magnificent beasts as 'queers' — Oh God!'" ("The Fabulous Kingdom of Gay Animals"). In *Biological Exuberance* Bagemihl writes, "Homosexual behavior occurs in more than 450 different kinds of animals worldwide, and is found in every major geographic region and every major animal group" (12). The main point here, of course, is that homosexual behavior is found in the natural world. If homosexual behavior is natural for animals, then we can justifiably assume that it is natural for human beings. After all, we are another species of animal, and if it were not natural for some — of course, not all — of us, then we would not see homosexuality among human beings.

Conclusion

I believe that same-sex marriage ought to be legal, and I hope that you agree that it ought to be legal, too. Of course, I am not advocating that churches ought to be forced to marry same-sex couples. I am simply saying that same-sex couples ought to be allowed by the government to have civil marriages. In doing so, same-sex married couples would have all the rights of opposite-sex married couples. In addition, they would be able to express their love and commitment to each other.

All of us should be as accepting of gays and lesbians as country music superstar Garth Brooks, whose sister is lesbian. Mr. Brooks made a pro-gay (and pro-freedom-of-religion) statement in his song "We Shall Be Free":

> When we're free to love anyone we choose,
> When this world's big enough for all different views,
> When we're all free to worship from our own kind of pew,
> Then we shall be free, (sing365.com)

Mr. Brooks also made a pro-love statement in that song, which celebrates love, whether it is between people of different races or people of the same sex. His sister helped educate Mr. Brooks, who is heterosexual, simply by being who she was. Mr. Brooks says, "The longer you live with it, the more you realize that it's just another form of people loving each other" (Wren 58-59).

Works Cited

Bagemihl, Bruce. *Biological Exuberance: Animal Homosexuality and Natural Diversity*. New York: St. Martin's Press, 1999. Print.

Belge, Kathy. "A Lesbian Marriage: I Wed My True Love." *Lesbian Life*. About.com, 2009. Web. 11 December 2009.

Brooks, Garth. Lyrics to "We Shall Be Free." Sing365.com. 2007. Web. 8 January 2010.

Ford, Michael Thomas. *Alec Baldwin Doesn't Love Me, and Other Trials from My Queer Life*. Los Angeles. CA: Alyson Books, 1998. Print.

Hay, Peter. *Canned Laughter*. New York: Oxford University Press, 1992. Print.

Helminiak, Daniel. *What the Bible Really Says About Homosexuality*. New Mexico: Alamo Square Press, 2002. Print.

Jost, Kenneth. "Gay Marriage: Should Same-Sex Unions Be Legally Recognized?" *CQ Researcher*. 5 September 2003. Web. 10 December 2009.

Lehrer, Jonah. "The Effeminate Sheep and Other Problems with Darwinian Sexual Selection." *Seed. Seed* Magazine. 2009. Web. 11 December 2009.

Leviticus. Holy Bible. King James Version. Electronic Text Center, University of Virginia Library. N.d. Web. 8 January 2010.

Lewis, C.S. *The Silver Chair*. New York: Macmillan Publishing Co., Inc., 1953. Print.

McCarthy, Susan. "The Fabulous World of Gay Animals." *Ivory Tower*. Salon, 2000. Web. 11 December 2009.

North, J. Lionel. "'Thou Shalt Commit Adultery' (Exod. 20:14, AV 1631): A First Survey of Alteration Involving Negatives in the Transmission of the Greek New Testament and of Early Church Responses to it." *The Journal of Theological Studies* 60(1) (2009): 22-69. Web. 12 January 2010.

Roughgarden, Joan. *Evolution's Rainbow: Diversity, Gender, and Sexuality in Nature and People*. Berkeley, University of California Press, 2004. Print.

United States Constitution. "First Amendment." *FindLaw*. Thomson Reuters, 2009. Web. 11 Dec. 2009.

Wren, Laura Lee. *Garth Brooks: Country Music Superstar*. Berkeley Heights, NJ: Enslow Publishers, Inc., 2002. Print.

Appendix E: About the Author

It was a dark and stormy night. Suddenly a cry rang out, and on a hot summer night in 1954, Josephine, wife of Carl Bruce, gave birth to a boy — me. Unfortunately, this young married couple allowed Reuben Saturday, Josephine's brother, to name their first-born. Reuben, aka "The Joker," decided that Bruce was a nice name, so he decided to name me Bruce Bruce. I have gone by my middle name — David — ever since.

Being named Bruce David Bruce hasn't been all bad. Bank tellers remember me very quickly, so I don't often have to show an ID. It can be fun in charades, also. When I was a counselor as a teenager at Camp Echoing Hills in Warsaw, Ohio, a fellow counselor gave the signs for "sounds like" and "two words," then she pointed to a bruise on her leg twice. Bruise Bruise? Oh yeah, Bruce Bruce is the answer!

Uncle Reuben, by the way, gave me a haircut when I was in kindergarten. He cut my hair short and shaved a small bald spot on the back of my head. My mother wouldn't let me go to school until the bald spot grew out again.

Of all my brothers and sisters (six in all), I am the only transplant to Athens, Ohio. I was born in Newark, Ohio, and have lived all around Southeastern Ohio. However, I moved to Athens to go to Ohio University and have never left.

At Ohio U, I never could make up my mind whether to major in English or Philosophy, so I got a bachelor's degree with a double major in both areas, then I added a Master of Arts degree in English and a Master of Arts degree in Philosophy. Yes, I have my MAMA degree.

Currently, and for a long time to come (I eat fruits and veggies), I am spending my retirement writing books such as *Nadia Comaneci: Perfect 10*, *The Funniest People in Dance*, *Homer's* Iliad: *A Retelling in Prose*, and *William Shakespeare's* Othello: *A Retelling in Prose*.

By the way, my sister Brenda Kennedy writes romances such as *A New Beginning* and *Shattered Dreams*.

Appendix F: Some Books by David Bruce

Discussion Guides Series

Dante's Inferno: *A Discussion Guide*

Dante's Paradise: *A Discussion Guide*

Dante's Purgatory: *A Discussion Guide*

Forrest Carter's The Education of Little Tree: *A Discussion Guide*

Homer's Iliad: *A Discussion Guide*

Homer's Odyssey: *A Discussion Guide*

Jane Austen's Pride and Prejudice: *A Discussion Guide*

Jerry Spinelli's Maniac Magee: *A Discussion Guide*

Jerry Spinelli's Stargirl: *A Discussion Guide*

Jonathan Swift's "A Modest Proposal": A Discussion Guide

Lloyd Alexander's The Black Cauldron: *A Discussion Guide*

Lloyd Alexander's The Book of Three: *A Discussion Guide*

Mark Twain's Adventures of Huckleberry Finn: *A Discussion Guide*

Mark Twain's The Adventures of Tom Sawyer: *A Discussion Guide*

Mark Twain's A Connecticut Yankee in King Arthur's Court: *A Discussion Guide*

Mark Twain's The Prince and the Pauper: *A Discussion Guide*

Nancy Garden's Annie on My Mind: *A Discussion Guide*

Nicholas Sparks' A Walk to Remember: *A Discussion Guide*

Virgil's Aeneid: *A Discussion Guide*

Virgil's "The Fall of Troy": A Discussion Guide

Voltaire's Candide: *A Discussion Guide*

William Shakespeare's 1 Henry IV: *A Discussion Guide*

William Shakespeare's Macbeth: *A Discussion Guide*

William Shakespeare's A Midsummer Night's Dream: *A Discussion Guide*

William Shakespeare's Romeo and Juliet: *A Discussion Guide*

William Sleator's Oddballs: *A Discussion Guide*

(*Oddballs* is an excellent source for teaching how to write autobiographical essays/personal narratives.)

Retellings of a Classic Work of Literature

Ben Jonson's The Alchemist: *A Retelling*

Ben Jonson's Bartholomew Fair: *A Retelling*

Ben Jonson's The Case is Altered: *A Retelling*

Ben Jonson's Catiline's Conspiracy: *A Retelling*

Ben Jonson's The Devil is an Ass: *A Retelling*

Ben Jonson's Epicene: *A Retelling*

Ben Jonson's Every Man in His Humor: *A Retelling*

Ben Jonson's Every Man Out of His Humor: *A Retelling*

Ben Jonson's The Fountain of Self-Love, or Cynthia's Revels: *A Retelling*

Ben Jonson's The New Inn: *A Retelling*

Ben Jonson's The Staple of News: *A Retelling*

Ben Jonson's Volpone, or the Fox: *A Retelling*

Christopher Marlowe's Complete Plays: Retellings

Christopher Marlowe's Dido, Queen of Carthage: *A Retelling*

Christopher Marlowe's Doctor Faustus: *Retellings of the 1604 A-Text and of the 1616 B-Text*

Christopher Marlowe's Edward II: *A Retelling*

Christopher Marlowe's The Massacre at Paris: *A Retelling*

Christopher Marlowe's The Rich Jew of Malta: *A Retelling*

Christopher Marlowe's Tamburlaine, Parts 1 and 2: *Retellings*

Dante's Divine Comedy: *A Retelling in Prose*

Dante's Inferno: *A Retelling in Prose*

Dante's Purgatory: *A Retelling in Prose*

Dante's Paradise: *A Retelling in Prose*

The Famous Victories of Henry V: *A Retelling*

From the Iliad *to the* Odyssey: *A Retelling in Prose of Quintus of Smyrna's* Posthomerica

George Peele: Five Plays Retold in Modern English

George Peele's The Arraignment of Paris: *A Retelling*

George Peele's The Battle of Alcazar: *A Retelling*

George Peele's David and Bathsheba, and the Tragedy of Absalom: *A Retelling*

George Peele's Edward I: *A Retelling*

George Peele's The Old Wives' Tale: *A Retelling*

George-A-Greene, The Pinner of Wakefield: A Retelling

The History of King Leir: *A Retelling*

Homer's Iliad: *A Retelling in Prose*

Homer's Odyssey: *A Retelling in Prose*

Jason and the Argonauts: A Retelling in Prose of Apollonius of Rhodes' Argonautica

The Jests of George Peele: *A Retelling*

John Ford: Eight Plays Translated into Modern English

John Ford's The Broken Heart: *A Retelling*

John Ford's The Fancies, Chaste and Noble: *A Retelling*

John Ford's The Lady's Trial: *A Retelling*

John Ford's The Lover's Melancholy: *A Retelling*

John Ford's Love's Sacrifice: *A Retelling*

William Shakespeare's Much Ado About Nothing: *A Retelling in Prose*
William Shakespeare's Othello: *A Retelling in Prose*
William Shakespeare's Pericles, Prince of Tyre: *A Retelling in Prose*
William Shakespeare's Richard II: *A Retelling in Prose*
William Shakespeare's Richard III: *A Retelling in Prose*
William Shakespeare's Romeo and Juliet: *A Retelling in Prose*
William Shakespeare's The Taming of the Shrew: *A Retelling in Prose*
William Shakespeare's The Tempest: *A Retelling in Prose*
William Shakespeare's Timon of Athens: *A Retelling in Prose*
William Shakespeare's Titus Andronicus: *A Retelling in Prose*
William Shakespeare's Troilus and Cressida: *A Retelling in Prose*
William Shakespeare's Twelfth Night: *A Retelling in Prose*
William Shakespeare's The Two Gentlemen of Verona: *A Retelling in Prose*
William Shakespeare's The Two Noble Kinsmen: *A Retelling in Prose*
William Shakespeare's The Winter's Tale: *A Retelling in Prose*

Children's Biography

Nadia Comaneci: Perfect Ten

Personal Finance

How to Manage Your Money: A Guide for the Non-Rich

Anecdote Collections

250 Anecdotes About Opera
250 Anecdotes About Religion
250 Anecdotes About Religion: Volume 2
250 Music Anecdotes
Be a Work of Art: 250 Anecdotes and Stories
Boredom is Anti-Life: 250 Anecdotes and Stories
The Coolest People in Art: 250 Anecdotes
The Coolest People in the Arts: 250 Anecdotes
The Coolest People in Books: 250 Anecdotes
The Coolest People in Comedy: 250 Anecdotes
Create, Then Take a Break: 250 Anecdotes
Don't Fear the Reaper: 250 Anecdotes
The Funniest People in Art: 250 Anecdotes
The Funniest People in Books: 250 Anecdotes
The Funniest People in Books, Volume 2: 250 Anecdotes
The Funniest People in Books, Volume 3: 250 Anecdotes
The Funniest People in Comedy: 250 Anecdotes
The Funniest People in Dance: 250 Anecdotes
The Funniest People in Families: 250 Anecdotes

The Funniest People in Families, Volume 2: 250 Anecdotes
The Funniest People in Families, Volume 3: 250 Anecdotes
The Funniest People in Families, Volume 4: 250 Anecdotes
The Funniest People in Families, Volume 5: 250 Anecdotes
The Funniest People in Families, Volume 6: 250 Anecdotes
The Funniest People in Movies: 250 Anecdotes
The Funniest People in Music: 250 Anecdotes
The Funniest People in Music, Volume 2: 250 Anecdotes
The Funniest People in Music, Volume 3: 250 Anecdotes
The Funniest People in Neighborhoods: 250 Anecdotes
The Funniest People in Relationships: 250 Anecdotes
The Funniest People in Sports: 250 Anecdotes
The Funniest People in Sports, Volume 2: 250 Anecdotes
The Funniest People in Television and Radio: 250 Anecdotes
The Funniest People in Theater: 250 Anecdotes
The Funniest People Who Live Life: 250 Anecdotes
The Funniest People Who Live Life, Volume 2: 250 Anecdotes
The Kindest People Who Do Good Deeds, Volume 1: 250 Anecdotes
The Kindest People Who Do Good Deeds, Volume 2: 250 Anecdotes
Maximum Cool: 250 Anecdotes
The Most Interesting People in Movies: 250 Anecdotes
The Most Interesting People in Politics and History: 250 Anecdotes
The Most Interesting People in Politics and History, Volume 2: 250 Anecdotes
The Most Interesting People in Politics and History, Volume 3: 250 Anecdotes
The Most Interesting People in Religion: 250 Anecdotes
The Most Interesting People in Sports: 250 Anecdotes
The Most Interesting People Who Live Life: 250 Anecdotes
The Most Interesting People Who Live Life, Volume 2: 250 Anecdotes
Reality is Fabulous: 250 Anecdotes and Stories
Resist Psychic Death: 250 Anecdotes
Seize the Day: 250 Anecdotes and Stories